A JOURNEY INTO THE MYSTICAL
INFLUENCING EVERYONE EVERYWHERE

WHY YOUR THOUGHTS AND FEELINGS MATTER

Ripples-A Journey into the Mystical

By John N Strachan

Editing by Cheri Jaques

Cover Design by Faeth Design

All rights reserved. This book may not be reproduced in whole or in part, or transmitted in any form, without written permission of the publisher. No part of this book may be reproduced, stored in a retrieval system, or transmitted in any form or by any means electronic, mechanical, photocopying, or recording, without written permission from the publisher.

Copyright © 2023

By John N Strachan

ISBN-979-8-9889646-0-5 (paperback)

ISBN-979-8-9889646-1-2 (hardback)

Acknowledgements

We all have areas of our lives where blessings are clearly recognized, and areas where the challenges can seem overwhelming. This book represents the completion of a vision, the manifestation of a project and perhaps the realization of my life's purpose.

It has only been with the help of friends, the support of loved ones, and the encouragement of those around me, that I can claim victory with the completion of this vision. I have such gratitude for Blanch Sharpenel, who encouraged me weekly as I struggled with the loss of my wonderful wife, keeping me on track to share these mystical stories. I wish many blessings for Cheri Jaques, a loving friend who read and edited my work, and offered such support and kind words through the whole process. My sister Suzanne Kennedy, called me every week encouraging me through some of the most difficult times.

I thank all of those that believed in me, my mother Dolores, my wife Cristina, my brother James, my brother in-law Rolando Diaz, Judy DeRosa, Anne Zuber, Lenny and Tiffany Markey, and Craig Harbarth. I thank Michael Faeth for his work on the cover design. I am also incredibly grateful for all of those that allowed me to place my hand on them for a reading. Each of them shared the most intimate parts of their being, allowing me to know and experience them on levels of heart and soul.

I thank all of those throughout time and space that have Rippled me and shared my Ripples.

Introduction

There are things that happen in life that can make us stop and question our understanding of reality. In fact it seems perhaps we should always be questioning what we think of as real, and why we so easily take certain things to be facts while totally discounting other ideas. What would happen if we made it a habit to see the world through the eyes of a child, and be amazed by everyday events?

This book was inspired by a number of factors, but without a doubt the passing of my wife the most wonderful life partner I could have ever hoped for was the catalyst that set everything in motion. She had been an amazing spiritual teacher, and it seemed that she just kept finding new ways to express and share love with all those around her. So many of my Mystical experiences involved our relationship, from the very beginning when we first met, and continued to her passing, and they still continue to this day.

After her passing, I needed to go through her files where I found many of her daily writings where she pondered thoughts, ideas and experiences. I had no idea that she had been such a prolific journaler. Perhaps the one thing that stood out the most was that she questioned everything! While most of us would accept an event at face value, she was always looking for a deeper meaning, a new perspective. It was obvious that there were many times that she was openly frustrated with herself, as if she absolutely knew that a higher truth was somehow eluding her. Her quest for greater understanding was such an amazing match for my own desire to know how everything works.

In most regards my life as a child and growing up was quite normal. My parents stayed together for the first 21 years of my life. I grew up with an older sister and a younger brother and we have always maintained a close bond. Perhaps what seemed to set me apart from my family and friends was my intense desire to understand how everything worked. I was the child that would take things apart just so I could make sense of how they operated. My father was a man that was a true "do it yourselfer," and I was always ready to help him. It would be many years before I would grasp that my desire to understand the workings of everything included Life itself.

As far back as I can remember, I was gifted with profound dreams, and the ability to recall most of them. As a child I did not understand that the creatures and demons that I often battled in my dreams were of my own making. I did not understand that even as a child I was very empathic. The witches, demons and creatures that I so often struggled with were in fact my way of processing the anger, guilt and fears of those around me. My father had been a kind yet often angry and sometimes violent man. He had been a paratrooper in WW2, and had witnessed and participated in some rather horrific events. As a child, how could I have possibly understood that I was feeling his emotions and trying to process them? Even though these dreams persisted for years, each one seemed so real, and I would be so lost in the emotions of the moment, that I did not recognize that regardless of the size and immense power of whatever creature I was battling, not one of them was ever actually able to harm me! Perhaps I had chosen this man to be my father, not in spite of his traumas, but because of those very issues. Perhaps learning to understand and process such things was a key part of learning more about how life works, how connected we all are, and it would help lead to the creation of this book.

Many years ago I remember hearing someone say that "What we are most afraid of is our own power." Part of me seemed to grasp this concept, yet it has only been during the last few years that the truth of the statement has become more apparent. It may seem like a silly idea that we could be afraid of our own abilities, however I have come to understand this concept from a much larger perspective. I used to believe that being afraid of my own power meant that I was afraid of doing great things even to the point of being Super Human. Now I see that just like I am the creator of every part of a dream, the character that seems to be me, the other people, animals, the landscape and even the circumstances of whatever is happening, I am also the creator of my life in this physical world! I am the one that chooses the people that surround me, the places that I go, the job that I have, and how I See and Feel about all of it! I am indeed the creator of my own reality, and that can be quite frightening. It is so much easier to point fingers and put blame on others for the difficulties that we face.

What if every part of our lives has been at the direction of the incredible power that we wield? What if every one of our challenges has been created by us and gives purpose to our lives? What if a perfect life did not include hitting a homerun every time, or having our very first love be our forever partner? What if it did not include having the most loving and perfect parents? What if it did not include landing the perfect job right out of school, but instead included things like striking out sometimes, or experiencing a broken heart, or having parents that forced us to rely on ourselves, and working many different jobs learning valuable lessons at each? What if the thing that we are really afraid of is that we are so powerful that we can create difficulties and situations that we believe we are unable to cope with them? What if we forget that just like in a dream where the creatures and demons cannot hurt us, so it is here in this reality also? What if every one of our choices not only affects us and our personal lives, but Ripples through the world changing everything for everyone?

I believe that we all have experiences in our lives that are meant to show that there is more to this physical realty than what would seem apparent. This book is about some of my personnel experiences that I would call Mystical or outside of what most people would think of as normal. I believe that we all have such experiences, but we often just brush them off as being weird. Most of this book is the telling of these mystical events, but it also includes some interesting thoughts on the science and physics of this physical reality.

Our days are filled with brand new moments, each giving us the opportunity to express our own unique vibration that we Ripple through eternity. Most of these precious moments we view as something that we need to get through until we reach a moment that we feel we can enjoy. For most of us we don't realize that every moment we are expressing ourselves and literally influencing everything, everywhere for everyone. We are not living for just the precious few rare moments that we find joyful. We are in fact sharing ourselves with the universe moment by moment whether we are experiencing joy, sorrow, fear or love.

"Ripples" is not just some fanciful fictional idea, it is a true perception of how physical life functions. A smile, a kind word, a helping hand, a look of recognition and gratitude, does not stop with the receiver of the gesture; it literally Ripples from that person through-out the community, the country, the world, the physical universe and perhaps even the dimensions beyond. Love is the highest of all vibrations, and it is always present, ready and excited to be Rippled by anyone willing to wield its power.

Table of contents

Story #1-Doodling
Recognizing deeper levels of communication

Story #2 Gymnastics
A glimpse into our physical potentials

Story #3-Life Underground
A face to face with a cute couple of ghosts

Story #4-My Journey Begins
Learning to meditate and meeting my guide

Story #5-Surrender, Awake or Asleep
Experiencing 2 realities simultaneously

Story #6-A Needle in a Haystack
The calling of a prized possession

Story #7-Who are you in the Void
When all that we know disappears

Story #8-A Chance to Stay
A very unusual Near Death Experience

Story #9-Orly
A gift from Spirit in a time of need

Story #10-What's Important?
A gift of insight from my guide

Story #11-Dimensional Healing
The class that stretched the boundaries of my reality

Story #12-Ayahuasca
My adventures beyond mind

Story #13-A Class in Consciousness
Discovering that Guilt, Anger, Fear, Love and Joy are more than just emotions

Story #14-The Eternal Now
Experiencing the Infinite moment

Story #15-The Meditation that Changed Me on Multiple Levels
The gift of experiencing Hell

Story #16-Resistance
How my body responded to years of Resistance

Story #17-The Quantum Self
A peek at the science of being human

Story #18-What is Everything Made Of?
Making sense of the physical universe

Story #19-Soul Song
We each have our own unique vibration

Story #20-Readings
Stories of an Empath

Story #21-Transformation
If you want something different, you must learn to be different

Story #22-What is Attention?
Discovering who we really are

Epilogue
Ripple by habit or ripple by choice

Story #1-Doodling

When I was 18 years old and still in high school, I had spent the first 3 years with a girl I knew I was in love with. She was just about five ft. tall, blonde, blue eyed and had such spunk. Little did I know then about the traumas that so many young girls have endured growing up. It would be decades before I would begin to understand the secret hurts that these young girls carried, the betrayals, the loss of self-esteem, the weight of a reality that a child can't know how to carry. Her past and circumstances at the time came to a head and one day she took it out on me, and suddenly we were no longer a couple. My senior year I found myself single, hurting and not wanting to be with any other girl.

Months after we had broken up, one of my teammates in gymnastics broke up with his girlfriend. She and I had been in an accelerated program for bright young minds. We had often worked together on class projects and along with several other friends from the same program would study together. It seemed a natural thing that she would call me after my friend broke up with her. We would sometimes talk for an hour or more, not about anything specific, just life.

One evening she was babysitting for people that I had never met and did not know in any way. She had put the kids to bed and then sat down and called me on the phone to chat. We talked about friends, and school, our parents and things that we would like to do. After about an hour, we were getting ready to say good night, when for some reason I mentioned that I had been doodling during most of our conversation. I had filled a page with patterns and images, many not making any sense. She asked me what I had drawn. I looked down at my masterpiece and I starting seeing how these lines and patterns actually looked like things. I told her that part of it looked like the shape of the United States. I could see the images of a whale, a horse, a cow and just kept describing items as I would see them.

When I was finished, she seemed quiet for a few moments, then she tells me that she has been sitting in this home office and looking at the adjacent wall all the time that we had been chatting. The wall had a very large map of the United States! There were whales swimming down the pacific coast! There were horses and cows, showing where ranching was prevalent! Everything I described from my doodle was what she had been looking at! We were both astonished and fascinated.

If only we could truly understand how we are all connected and all the ways we are capable of communicating. How often do we pick up thoughts and feelings from other people and not recognize that they are not our own. In this case we had been chatting on the phone, and I was somehow able to pick up unspoken thoughts, but could we have communicated by just thinking of the other person without even being on the phone? If a friend or family member is going through a traumatic event, do they send out messages that we might somehow pick up?

During another of our phone chats we were again getting ready to say goodnight, when she tells me that she had just finished baking cookies. She says, guess how many I baked? Without missing a beat, I said seventy-nine and one half. She said no way! That was the exact amount! She did not have enough dough for a final whole cookie, and so made a half cookie and the total was seventy-nine and one half!

For whatever reason we seemed to be connected in ways that I may never understand. We never had a relationship other than being good friends. Even though I've had a number of girlfriends I never had this type of non-verbal communication with any of them that I was ever aware of.

Even now as I write about her, I feel that there is some type of connection with her.

A few years later I had moved about four hours away into a small mountain community. I lived and worked there for about 15 years, and I had not seen this girl for many years. I had become a general contractor and worked mostly on doing remodel work. I had completed several jobs for an older gentleman and his wife, and he had called me back to give an estimate on some additional work. My wife and I had become friends with this couple, so my wife accompanied me there to look at the job. As we sat and visited, the man mentioned his daughter in the Bay Area and said her name. I looked at him and asked if this was the same girl that went to my high school and was in this accelerated program. It turned out that this man was indeed her father. I had become friends with her father, whom I had never met while living in the San Francisco Bay Area. Somehow there seemed to be ties with this family that I will probably only understand when I get to the other side of the veil.

Story #2-Gymnastics

In my sophomore year in high school, I joined the gymnastic team. Gymnastics at my high school was a fairly new sport, and at first it was taught by a physical education instructor that had almost no experience with gymnastics. He soon quit and the program would have been dropped if not for the tennis instructor, who very courageously volunteered to step in. Some of the team had started a year or two prior to my arrival, so it was great that there were at least a few with some experience. It was somewhat out of my comfort zone to join in a sport that I knew nothing about. As with probably all teenagers, I wanted to fit in and feel accepted by my peers. For me, the two things that I was most afraid of, were looking stupid and getting hurt. Gymnastics offered the opportunity to look stupid and get hurt at the same time. Yet here I was, choosing to participate and facing those fears.

I had joined the team after watching a couple of the guys doing routines on floor exercise. Watching a tumbling pass with flips and twists looked awesome! I soon found out that just about every individual move came with the potential of injury or at least a lot of sore muscles. What I had not thought about, was that gymnastics was more than just floor exercise. We were expected to practice on all of the equipment. This included the pommel horse, high bar, still rings, parallel bars and the vaulting horse. Each apparatus came with its own unique set of required skills.

On one of the first days of practice, we were working on the still rings. We started with an inlocate, which is one of the most basic moves. I found this to be something that I was good at right away. In fact, my very first inlocate was better than most the guys that had been working the rings for awhile. A few days later, we were back at the rings and practicing a dislocate. This move seemed much more difficult, even though it is still one of the most basic moves. I was afraid to even try it.

That night I had one of my vivid dreams. I was on the rings and getting ready to attempt a dislocate. As I began with the proper swing and raised my legs, folding them close to my chest and keeping them straight, I felt every muscle and understood how my body needed to move. I completed the dislocate with such ease and grace. It felt awesome! The next day after school, I was back in the gym for practice. When it was my turn I jumped up and grabbed the rings. Without hesitation, I performed a beautiful dislocate just like in my dream. I felt every muscle just as I had the night before.

Most of my progress in gymnastics came with a lot of practice, lots of attempts, many fails, but slow progress. One of the best parts of gymnastics was that everybody helped everybody. Everyone was always willing to offer advice, be a "spotter," or show you how to do a move. It was always about competing with yourself to get better, everyone advanced at their own pace.

In my senior year, we were all practicing an iron cross on the rings. We had taken a bicycle inner tube and cut it, making a rubber rope out of it. We would wrap one end on each ring and then lift our feet into the part that was hanging. As we lowered our bodies into the cross position, the tube would hold some of our weight. It was a great way to practice, but it was far from actually being able to hold a legitimate cross. There were a number of my teammates that were much stronger than I was, but no one was even close to holding a cross.

Then one night, another vivid dream, I was on the rings and preparing to lower myself into the cross. Just like 2 years earlier with the dislocate, as I lowered myself, I felt every muscle. As I lowered to the point that I would always give up, I felt myself go beyond where I had ever gone. As I passed that point, the words, "this is child's play", went through my mind. I reached the position of a perfect cross and all I could think, was this is child's play. In fact, it was so easy holding the cross that I thought I could bring my legs up into the L position. I lifted my legs, and there I was holding a beautiful cross with my legs in a perfect L. Again, I thought this is child's play! I thought that I could keep this L position and raise myself back above the rings. As I began to raise up, there seemed to be no strength involved. It was again, child's play to pull back above the rings. Through all of this, I felt every muscle and understood how the body needed to move.

The next day, I could not wait for school to end and to get back on the rings. This combination of moves that I had accomplished in my dream was on the level of what a good gymnast in college might be able to do, not some little guy like me in high school. The final bell rang and I headed to the gym. After everyone had arrived, the coach went over a few things, and then let us practice whatever we wanted to. I of course headed to the rings. I had to wait my turn, being third in line. I watched each of the two in front of me as they practiced moves that they hoped to put in their competition routine. I also helped spot each of them and helped with their dismounts.

My turn, I jumped up and grabbed onto the rings. I started with a couple of dislocates and easy moves, then pulled myself up above the rings. It felt so similar to the dream as I began to lower down into a cross. I reached the spot that I had never been able to go beyond and just as in the dream, I felt every muscle as I lowered into a perfect cross! As I held the position, the thought went through my mind, "this is child's play." I had already lived this experience in the dream and already knew that I could raise my legs into the L position, which I did with ease. It is difficult to put into words, the incredible freedom that I was experiencing. It felt as if reality no longer had me in control, but I was in control of my reality. By now the entire team, including the coach were all standing nearby and watching. After a few seconds, while continuing to hold the L position, I pulled my body back above the rings! Every bit of it was "child's play."

To say that those watching were surprised would be a huge understatement. There were guys on the team much stronger than me and for them, what I had just done made no sense. From my experience, strength was not even an issue. I did not feel like there was much of an effort needed as I went through the individual moves. Just to be sure, during practice that day, I tried repeating the series of moves and each time I found it to be child's play.

The next day, the coach asked me to try it again, he wanted to watch exactly how each move was performed. He wanted to see my hand position and where my elbows were facing, back or up. He wanted to see if my arms were locked straight out and not bent. I jumped up on the rings and repeated my performance from the day before. It almost seemed as if the coach was looking for some way to invalidate what he had witnessed.

The following day during practice, I went through the moves a couple more times, but for some reason on this day, I felt like I needed to put effort and strength into each of the moves. I was still able to get through them, but it was no longer child's play. On the fourth day, I found that I was not able to even hold a cross, I was bending my arms and using every bit of strength that I could find, but was unable to hold the cross position. I tried many times after that, but was never able to hold a cross again. For three days, it was child's play, and then the magic was gone.

It's my belief that my coach and teammates' beliefs that I should not be able to perform these moves, became stronger in my reality, than my own actual experience of it. I bought into their beliefs and let mine go. This was a mystical experience that I have shared for decades. I have often pondered over the limitations that we buy into, just because so many others believe in those limitations. What kinds of things could we accomplish if we were not held back by what the masses believe?

Story #3-Life Underground

Growing up, it had been one of my chores to clean up the piles of poop from the two German Shepards that we had. About once a week I would dig a hole and bury the piles. One day as I looked around the yard I thought about how at some point I would run out of places to dig these holes. The thought came to me, "What if I dig a really big, deep hole that I can just keep filling for awhile." It seemed like such a good idea. I started digging this hole and was thrilled that it just kept getting deeper. As I was working away on my project, my younger brother came out to see what I was up to. He was so impressed with the depth of the hole he asked if I could make it a little bigger so he could climb into it. After a little more work, he was able to fit into the hole. As I looked at him down in the hole I decided to make the hole big enough for both of us. At some point dreams and imagination took over and the hole kept growing. The digging went on for days and then weeks! As the hole became too deep to lift dirt out of, I would fill several five gallon buckets of dirt, lift the handles so they were pointing upwards and then climb out of the hole. I would take a rope that I had tied a hook onto and I would swing the hook to catch one of the bucket handles. After pulling each of the buckets out, I would dump them in the yard and do the process all over again.

When the digging was finally done, I was the proud owner of an eight foot by ten foot by ten foot deep hole! My father had a contractor friend that was so impressed with my project that he donated all of the lumber and plastic sheeting I needed to build a room underground. I poured a concrete floor and lined the hole with a waterproof plastic sheeting. I built walls and a very strong ceiling that I then covered with about two feet of dirt. I left a three foot by three foot opening in the ceiling that allowed me to construct a ladder that dropped straight down into my room. I then built a small shed over the opening to insure that my access was water tight. I installed carpeting, electrical outlets, a phone line and an intercom to the house.

I had started this project while I was in the eighth grade and finished it about a year later while I was in high school. I moved out of the house and into my underground room. Even during midday, I could turn my lights off and it would be completely dark. I could not see my hand in front of my face. The ground acted as insulation and the room maintained a pretty consistent temperature of around seventy degrees. The silence was amazing! There were no sounds from outside the room and unlike being in the house, there were no sounds from the refrigerator or washing machine. There was not even the sound of someone walking around the house, just silence.

Being in high school, I have to admit that I had a lot of small parties in that room. I also have to admit that sleeping alone in such a dark quiet place took some getting used to. It was surprising to notice how loud my own breathing was, and even my heartbeat seemed to echo in my ears. Sometimes I would wake up in the middle of the night and not remember where I was, and without any light I couldn't see my surroundings.

I had been sleeping in my underground room for several months when I awoke one night to an unusual sound. When I say unusual, I mean any sound was unusual since normally there was only silence. I strained to try and identify what the sound was and where it might be coming from. It seemed to be someone whispering and it seemed to be coming from the upper corner of my room. The sound was so soft that I could not tell what the voice was saying. I eventually fell back asleep. In the morning I thought about the whispers but then went about my day.

The next night, I was once again awakened by the strange whisper. I looked around the room and only saw darkness. I turned on the light and the whisper disappeared. I was alone in the room! This time the whisper had seemed to be a little louder, but I still could not make out any words. This pattern went on for the next several nights, each time waking me up between one and two in the morning. Each time the whisper was getting a little louder and then one night I began to make out not only actual words, but I could tell that they were being spoken by two young children. One of the voices seemed to be from a very young boy, and he was evidently interested in my being there in the room. The other voice seemed to be from what I believed was this boy's sister who sounded a little older.

Each night I would wake up between one and two o'clock and each night the voices became clearer. This went on for about a week and a half, and then one night when I was again awakened by the whispers, I opened my eyes to the sight of two foggy distorted images up in the corner of the room! I still could not see my hand in front of my face, nor any part of the room, but I could see two small clouds of light right where the whispers were coming from.

I did not have a bed in the room and instead slept on the carpeted floor. I had installed a nice thick carpet pad so the entire floor was my bed. I always slept with my head at the opposite wall from where the ladder went up to the shed above. Since I was always in this same spot, it was easy to picture where the voices were coming from. Much in the same way that the voices had become clearer over a period of days, the foggy images became clearer each night. Then one night as I opened my eyes, I could clearly see these two young children. The boy appeared to be around two to three years old and the girl somewhere around the age of four or five. This time they were standing close to the ladder at the opposite wall from where my head was and probably just three feet from where my feet were. I could tell that the boy wanted to walk over to me, but his sister was holding him back. I'm not sure if they were actually talking or if I was somehow hearing their thoughts.

After a couple of nights of seeing them next to the ladder, it felt as though we were all getting used to seeing each other. The next night when they came to visit, I was lying there feeling comfortable about their presence, and they seemed to be more at ease also. This time as the boy began to move towards me, his sister did not stop him. He moved to where he was just next to my lower leg and knelt down and gently put his hand on my leg just below my knee. Instantly the spot that he touched tingled and felt almost numb at the same time. It wasn't an unpleasant feeling, but it caught me by surprise. Touching me seemed to somehow give this little boy comfort and I was moved at seeing how much this simple act had meant to him. Then the little girl moved over and knelt next to my other leg and touch me just as her brother had done. Instantly I felt the same tingle and numbness. Just like her brother, this little girl seemed to take such comfort in touching me. They each let out a little giggle.

It had taken more than two weeks from the first time that I heard their whispers to get to this point of physical contact. It was almost as though it needed to happen so slowly so that all three of us could be somewhat at ease with each other. The next several nights were more of the same with the children getting a little bolder each time. They were moving around me and touching me with joy. Although I could hear them speaking to each other, I believe that it was not audible sound but more like I was hearing their thoughts. There was never a point where I actually spoke to them.

One day I shared with two of my best friends that there was something unusual happening in my room, and I invited them to come and spend a night there with me. Dennis and Danny arrived early, and we sat down in the room telling jokes and remembering silly things that we used to do. High school was a good time for me, with lots of friends and people to share fun times with. Dennis and Danny were two friends that I had spent a lot of time with. The evening went by quickly and it was finally time to turn off the light and go to sleep. We lay side by side with our heads at the same wall that I always had my head. I was quite used to the complete darkness, but I could feel that my friends were a little uneasy. I had not given them any information as to what unusual things might be happening in the room and for some reason they had not asked either. After awhile we all fell asleep.

Just as had happened each previous night, I awoke to the sound of whispers. I was surprised to also hear Danny whispering to Dennis. Danny had been the first to hear the whispers from the upper corner of the room and had already nudged Dennis to wake him up too. Now all three of us were awake and all three of us were hearing the voices. I could tell that my friends were getting anxious, so I let them know that it was all okay, that this is what I had invited them here to experience. I instructed them to lie quietly and just listen. I wanted to know if they would be able to hear actual words and would we each hear the same things.

As we lay there, the whispers turned into audible voices almost as though they had started from far away and were getting closer until they finally entered the room. As we all listened, both of my friends validated that we were all hearing the very same words and that they were the voices of two young children. Needless to say, we were all wide awake but we had not changed our positions and were still lying down. Then just as had become the "norm," the foggy apparitions appeared in the upper corner of the room and then slowly moved to the spot near the bottom of the ladder. The figures became more defined and brighter until the two children stood at our feet looking like beings made of light.

Both Danny and Dennis had been quiet while this had transpired, but now they began to whisper and again validate that we were all seeing the very same thing. They each described the children, from their height, ages, positions in the room and what they appeared to be wearing. Surprisingly both of my friends seemed almost gleeful to be witnessing the appearance of these two children. Perhaps because they were so young and seemed so unthreatening we were all very relaxed. Then the young boy stepped forward towards Danny and knelt down next to him and put his hand on his leg. I heard Danny lightly gasp and I knew that he was feeling the very same tingling that I had always experienced.

It was strange that the glow of the children somehow illuminated the room. I could see my friends and I could see the young boy kneeling next to Danny. Then the young girl moved towards Dennis and touched his hand and just as Danny had done, Dennis let out a gentle gasp.

The children only stayed a few minutes, but it was enough to keep my friends and me up for an hour talking about the experience. This was the only time that the children appeared while I had guests in the room. I am not sure why these two children were there and why they were so interested in me. I was sixteen when this all happened, and all I can say is that it was one in a long line of mystical experiences that I have been blessed with. They have helped me to question what is real. By the age of eighteen I had developed a real passion and desire to understand reality.

I understood that a dream seemed to be totally real while I was experiencing it. I understood that "normal life" seemed to be real while I was awake, and I also understood that I could get lost in my imagination to the point where even what was in my mind seemed to be real. Somehow it seemed that at certain times in my life, cracks would appear that would allow these different realities to bleed into one another. The one thing that I knew for certain was that reality had to be so much bigger than anyone had ever explained to me.

Story #4-My Journey Begins

In high school, I had the opportunity to take a class called supernatural literature. This class opened my eyes to the possibility that "reality" might be quite different than I had imagined. I was like a sponge, reading book after book. One that particularly spoke to me was titled "Seth Speaks" by Jane Roberts. This book was supposedly written word for word as a disincarnate being spoke through Jane Roberts. It answered questions that I had long wondered about. It brought up new questions concerning the natural or un-natural abilities that we all might have. Both my parents had been raised Catholic, but no longer believed in that teaching. They never took me to church, and my father would tell me that "there is no God, if you believe in God it's because you are afraid." He was sure after serving in WW2 that no God would allow such things to happen. You live, you die and that's all there is.

I found myself wandering the field behind our house just about every morning around 2:00 AM. I pondered what my father said, and I thought, if he is right and there is no God, what do I do with my life? What is important? If this is all there is, should I do whatever I feel like? Should I be the nicest person I could be? Do I try and make as much money as possible? Should I become someone important and powerful? Then I thought, if my father is wrong, and there is more to life, all those same questions still apply. Why am I here? What is important? Who am I?

I began meditating every day. It was a struggle at first. I had read some books on meditation techniques, but never had any personal training. I tried clearing my mind, to have no thoughts. I didn't realize at the time that this is actually an advanced type of meditation. It is far easier to focus on breathing, or a mantra, or some verse, rather than stopping all thought, and just having a clear mind. Then I read a book about self-hypnosis. How much like meditation this sounded. I began to combine the technique used in hypnosis of visualizing walking down stairs and matching my breaths as I descended. During a trip to the pacific coast of California, I had found an amazing set of stairs that had been carved into the side of a cliff and next to them was a small creek. As I descended the stairs, there would be a flat path for a few feet, or sometimes a couple of yards, and then more stairs. At the bottom, the stairs and the creek were side by side and both going through a fifteen foot high rock archway that then opened onto a large beach and the Pacific Ocean. It was amazing, like something out of a fairy tale.

This was the perfect set of stairs to visualize in my meditations. I would get comfortable and sit with my legs crossed. With my eyes closed, I would take three deep calming breaths. I would then see myself standing at the top of the stairs. I would take one step down while breathing out and say to myself "deeper, deeper, down, down." After taking ten of these steps down, I would picture that I was standing on one of the flat landings and I would slowly turn and look back up to the top of the stairs. This helped to confirm in my mind that I was not in the same place I had started from, and that I was indeed going deeper into relaxation. Then I would turn and do another ten steps down, just repeating the process. As I reached the bottom, I would walk through the rock archway, and onto the beautiful beach.

By the time I had reached the bottom of the stairs and stepped onto the beach, I was always in an altered state of consciousness. This technique consistently brought me into my deepest, most profound meditations. One day, upon reaching the beach and feeling as though I had let everything go, I felt that I was not alone. I looked around and saw only the open beach, the ocean and the rock cliffs above. Still, there was a knowing that I was not alone in this place of solitude that I had created in my mind. I understood that I was in meditation and that this was a place in my imagination, so who could find me here?

In my mind, I asked the question, "Who are you?" Then in front of me, there appeared what I would describe as a distortion of air or space. Something like looking through a light cloud of steam. It was between me and the ocean, but I knew that this was the energy that had come into my private space. I could sense that this was not an energy I needed to be afraid of, and I somehow also knew that this energy had always been with me. When I say always, I felt like that meant not just this lifetime, and not just all my physical incarnations, but always as in eternity. It was almost as though I were standing next to my bodiless self. Without any words spoken, information was being brought to my awareness. I say it this way, because everything that I was being made aware of seemed like I already knew, yet somehow I just didn't know it consciously.

It's been many years since that first conscious contact with my guide. For a long time, it was necessary to descend all the stairs and onto the beach in order to reach a level where I could communicate with him. Now I know that he is always there in every moment, and it is just a matter of tuning my awareness to meet his vibration. Now, I no longer need the stairs or the beach and it generally takes only seconds to be with him. I can ask any question and he is there to answer. I have pondered thousands of questions and listened to his view on all of them. For the most part, the answers that I have received have been so different than I was expecting. It seems obvious to me that his point of view is vastly larger than my own personal view point.

He explained that as a (Perceived) physical, flesh and blood being in this reality, all we have is a point of view. It doesn't matter what we are looking at, we can only see it from our own limited perspective. If I were to hold up my cell phone in just the perfect position so that all you could see was the bottom strip, and then ask you to describe what you see; you might describe it as a black plastic strip about three and half inches in length, and a little less than a half an inch wide. While this description is quite accurate from that specific point of view, someone standing to my side would be looking at the screen of the phone and would have a completely different description. If you pictured this phone floating in the middle of a large room and then imagined a large sphere, (the size of the room) surrounding the phone, and this sphere being made up of an almost infinite number of dots or points. Each point would have a unique view of the phone, some being quite similar, but most being very different. No matter which point you view the phone from, your description may be accurate as it relates to that point of view, but when you change where you stand, the view changes and your understanding of what you are seeing changes. Using the example of the sphere, we can see that there are almost an unlimited number of angles in which to view the phone from, but we have only been looking from the outer layer of the sphere. When we understand that the phone or object can not only be viewed from different angles, but also from an unlimited number of distances, from up close to so far away that the object may become too small to even detect; then we can finally see that there are literally infinite points in which to stand and view from. No matter which point we view from, we can never see the entire phone. Even if somehow we could see from multiple points, we still could not see the inner workings of the phone; we would still only be looking at the surface. This is the case for every object, person, situation or even idea. We can never see the entire truth of anything.

Besides our view changing when we move to a different position, our emotional state also influences how we see everything. If we are feeling angry or upset, our view of a situation would be quite different than if we were to be feeling love or joy.

If you could perceive the phone in its entirety, from all points of view at once, there could be no sense of separation. You would no longer be you and the phone be the phone. There could only be the awareness of how we are all connected. This would be true of everything, not just the phone. If you were to look at a piece of paper and could know everything, perceive everything about that piece of paper, you would have to understand how it could even exist! You would know how it is made up of trillions of atoms and you would have to know what formed those atoms. You would have to understand what magic told those atoms to become a piece of paper. You would have to understand that you are perceiving the paper and in order to understand that, you would have to understand who and what you are that makes it possible for you to perceive the paper. If indeed you could understand who the perceiver is, the secrets of the universe would be revealed. You would have to know what your place is in the universe, whether you are separate from everything or part of everything or perhaps even the creator of all that is. Just to know a piece of paper in its totality would be to lose your point of view and become both the viewed and the viewer.

As we look at the "Reality" of "Reality," we see that there is nothing that we know in totality. All we have is a point of view and our point of view will always be unique to us. No one has ever in the history of the world, seen the world like you do. No one will ever see the world the same way that you see it. It is not possible for anyone else to see or experience the world like you do. I have so much more to say about this, but we will look at it later.

In this journey with my guide, I have never asked if he had a name. In fact, I never asked if he was a he. I sense a male energy, but there is also the female energy. I only refer to my guide as a "he." Also, I have never felt that his energy is separate from mine. It has never felt like he is someone else talking with me. It is more like he is an extension of me or that I am a part of him, or perhaps we are the same being with one outside the "veil" and one behind it. Over the years, no question has been off limits, except for specific questions regarding specific people. There have been times where I have asked about a difficulty that a friend or client might be experiencing and received the "feeling" that it was not appropriate for the answer to be divulged. For the past several years, my go-to question has been "What is it that I most need to know or remember right now?" With this question, I never know where it's going to take me and I am sitting with excitement at what might come next.

This is what has led me to start writing his answers to some of the more intriguing questions as I have become so driven to investigate and understand better what it is to be human. Is there a purpose to being here? Is there a God? If there is a God, am I of value to that God? What in this physical reality is of actual value? Is it even possible to find out or understand these things?

I understand that religions are supposed to answer these questions, and yet answers are in words and words are subject to interpretation. Someone declares that God is infinite. We take it for granted that we know what that means, but have you ever pondered what infinity really is? Can our minds grasp such a concept? Scientists say that atoms are mostly space and energy, and we take it for granted that we know what space is and we know what energy is. If you are having a dream and in that dream you are looking into the vastness of space with trillions of stars, does that dream take up space? Is your created universe just in your mind, or does it occupy some area of space? Does the act of creating or perceiving the stars in your dream take energy? Are the stars made of energy? What is energy? Is it possible for us to even know such things with our limited points of view?

One day, my wife and I were having a session with a spiritual teacher. The teacher asked me how I felt about my wife. I immediately replied that I loved her. He then asked if I would be willing to let go of that point of view and rescind any commitments to it? I said, why would I do that? Isn't love the greatest thing? He soon got me to understand that Love like all words, is just a word, subject to infinite interpretations. He helped me to understand, that if I could let go of my very limited point of view of what Love was, that the actual experience of Love could be so much greater than anything I could have imagined, and that behaviors and actions that I would not have included in my interpretation of Love, could actually be part of Love, and in fact perhaps there are no actions that could be separate from Love. Ever since that session I have been much more aware of the limitedness of words. We use them constantly to communicate with each other and to describe everything, yet their very use limits every description!

If I were to look at a rose and then describe it in words, I might say things like it is red, it has petals and a stem. I could mention the size, the shape, the fragrance, yet no matter how many words I use I could never get someone to actually experience the rose. I could only get them to form a limited picture in their imagination and it would have no life or energy to it. Even if somehow I was able to describe the rose in such a way that my descriptions could make someone able to experience the rose, it would still only be experienced from one point of view and never in its totality.

If every point of view is accurate when viewed in that very particular way and from that particular point, but could NEVER be the entire truth, then how important is it that we hold on to our points of view as though our lives depended on them? How invested are we in the need to be RIGHT? What if we could actually acknowledge that every point of view has some level of truth or accuracy? Could it be possible that our point of view is never wrong, but always limited?

Story #5-Surrender, Awake or Asleep

It was a quiet morning in 1980, I was taking a nap on the couch in the living room. My parents had divorced several years prior, so I had moved back into the house to help care for my mother and my younger brother. Life at the time seemed relatively easy. I was managing a restaurant and making a good income. I had a wonderful girlfriend and I enjoyed life with my mother and brother.

As I lay sleeping on the couch I slowly became aware of sounds coming from the kitchen. They seemed far away almost as though they were not quite connected to my reality. The sounds somehow awakened my conscious mind to being aware of the dream that I was having. I was in a conflict with some sort of creature that appeared to be mostly a human male but also possessed some animal qualities. I knew that we had been in several battles and neither of us seemed to be able to get the upper hand over the other.

At the point where I became conscious in the dream, I was trying to escape the conflict. I was running down a street and this creature/man was chasing me. I could sense that I was running not because I was afraid, but rather that I had realized that the battle was unwinnable for either of us. It just didn't make sense to continue the silly dance of conflict.

Again I became aware of the sounds in the kitchen. I knew that it was my mother and brother whispering to each other trying not to bother my sleep. Somehow their whispers had awakened my conscious mind so that I was totally aware of lying on the couch in the living room and listening to them and yet I was also still in my dream and being chased by this dark soul.

I had experienced "lucid" dreaming before, but this was the first time that I seemed to be totally conscious in both the awake and dream states. I could have easily decided to put all my attention on my mother and brother and left the dream behind. I could have also chosen to focus on the dream and be consumed only by its reality. Instead I stayed in both worlds, letting the dream continue and listening to the voices in the kitchen.

I could feel how much I loved my mother and brother, and I was in such gratitude for having them in my life. I could feel how my conflict with this creature in my dream had been so silly. I became so awake in the dream that I knew that it was a dream and that I could do anything that I wanted in it. I looked up into the sky and launched myself upwards, leaving the creature behind. I was soaring over the houses and buildings, looking down at the streets and the lawns and the trees. I was feeling such joy and such freedom that being chased by that man was a distant memory. My dream had turned from one of conflict to one of such raw pleasure just by adding a dose of awareness and understanding.

After flying for awhile I was ready to turn my attention back to the kitchen and a different reality. I opened my eyes, being greeted by the living room. It almost felt like everything in it was welcoming me back to its reality. Even the daylight filling the room felt like it was embracing me with a warm hug and saying welcome back. I got up from the couch and stretched my body feeling so content. I joined my mother and brother in the kitchen. It is difficult to describe the amount of love that I was feeling for them and for life, but I think the smile on my face was saying it all. They both looked at me wondering what on earth I could have been up to that I was feeling so good.

It's so interesting thinking that just minutes earlier I had been in a dark dream. I was in mortal combat with a creature that seemed so powerful that nothing I did could even harm it. No matter what I hit this creature with it would just laugh and keep coming at me. Then with a dose of awareness I understood that he could not actually harm me either. It became obvious that the best way to deal with this creature was to surrender to the fact that I did not need to do battle with it. By becoming awake enough I was able to find a way out of the battle that literally lifted up and into such a beautiful sky. The once powerful creature had been reduced to a distant memory that held no power over me. If only I had understood the significance of this dream. If I could have seen way back then that so many battles in my life did not have to be fought.

In a matter of a few minutes I had gone from being in a battle to flying over the most amazing landscape with such freedom, and then to placing my attention back to the kitchen where my mother and brother were speaking so softly to each other. The battle had seemed so real. My decision to escape the conflict and fly above into the freedom of the sky had seemed so real, and now standing in the kitchen with my family seemed so real. Who is to say what constitutes reality? Is reality only a point of view? Or does our view of reality change according to where we are standing?

Is it possible that even in this so called "physical reality" that we could turn away from a conflict and focus on something quite positive? Could we train ourselves or educate ourselves on how to make more positive choices? Could life literally become more joyful just by making better choices? Standing in the kitchen and feeling so much love for my mother and brother made me wonder why I did not always experience this deep love for them. I always understood that I loved them, but why was this time so different? They had not done anything in particular to cause me to feel more love. Why was I suddenly in such a state of appreciation for having them in my life? As I pondered this, I realized that in my dream I had surrendered the need for conflict and had gone from resisting what was happening to embracing a new and more expansive reality, flying above into a higher state of being. It had been this act of surrender that had changed my experience of life in the moment and allowed me to remember the deeper appreciation and love that I always had for my family.

We have been taught that when there is a conflict we should fight harder in order to overcome the situation, but what if other options are available? What if the option to let go of the conflict is possible? What if the conflict can only exist when looked at or viewed through the eyes of fear, anger or pride? What if the same situation were to be viewed through higher levels of awareness, such as acceptance, reason or love? Often during a conflict, we see the possibility that we as humans stand to be diminished if we were to lose the battle. We begin learning as children if we are given a toy, we somehow see that toy as belonging to us and it even becoming an extension of who we are. If that toy is taken away it feels as though part of us has been taken also. We feel diminished, less than we were when we possessed that toy. So it seems that as adults, losing a conflict feels like we have been diminished, when in fact it is only the egoic mind that sees itself as diminished. The true self has not been changed or diminished. In fact, I believe that it is not possible to actually be diminished, it is only possible to feel diminished. If this is really the case, then who is feeling or experiencing the feeling of being diminished? Who is aware of the feeling? The obvious answer would be to say that "I" am the one that is aware of how I feel. I am the one that lost the conflict or the possession and now I must be less than I was before this thing was lost. Certainly looking at the situation through the eyes or vibration of fear, the loss would be felt or experienced in a particular way, but when standing or viewing from the vibration of love, the loss would feel or be experienced in a completely different way. In both cases, it was still the "I" that was perceiving the situation, yet the feeling or experience was vastly different depending on which vibration we were viewing from.

This experience of the dual awareness of the dream taking place and the awareness of my family in the kitchen, two realities happening at the same time, truly changed my perception of what is real. Reality is always dependent on where we are standing. I am referring to "standing" as not just location, but more importantly, the vibration that we are viewing from.

Story #6-A Needle in a Haystack

All during my childhood, my father had told stories of the jeep club that he had been a member of. He and my mother used to love the trips up into the mountains, four wheeling and camping at different mountain lakes. He and his friends would often go deer hunting with bows and arrows. They took pride in hunting without guns. One of the men in the club had become an expert on making hunting knives. He would often show off his latest creation, to the oos and ahs of the group. On one of the camping trips, my father asked this man to teach him how to make a knife for himself. The master knife maker agreed and invited my father over to his shop where they could come up with a unique design.

I'm not sure how many days they worked together, or how long it took, but the knife was finally completed. This was all before I was born, but as I grew up, I was moved by how proud my father was of that knife. I never saw him use it, and he had stopped hunting by the time I was born. He did however love to show it off. Every time he had a new friend over to the house, out came this magnificent knife. It was beautiful, with a steel blade on one side and saw teeth on the back. The handle was made of bone that had been worked into the perfect fit for his hand.

When I graduated from high school, my father felt that I was now a man and gifted me this prized possession. Knowing what it meant to him, made it so special to me, that I treasured it. I kept it in a drawer and only pulled it out once in awhile to show it off, or to just hold it. A couple of years later, I took my younger brother who was thirteen at the time, on his first backpacking trip up in the Sierra National Forest. I had to bring my knife of course. We parked the car at a reservoir and grabbed our back packs.

After about two miles of hiking in an area that I was somewhat familiar with, having backpacked there with friends from high school, we crossed a large creek by rock hopping big boulders. The creek was fast moving to our right side, but at the boulders where we were crossing, there was a waterfall that dropped about twenty feet. Instead of the water flowing over the boulders, it was finding its way through the boulders, creating a roar of power as it fell the twenty feet below us. As we headed up the mountain from the creek, we were in uncharted territory. I had never been beyond the creek before. The mountain side was steep, so our path was diagonal and sometimes switchback as we made our way higher. The farther up we went, the fewer trees there were and the view began to get spectacular.

Looking ahead and across the side of the mountain, in the direction that we had intended to go, the entire mountainside appeared to be covered with dense Manzanita bushes. From where we were, there was no visible path through what looked to be miles of bushes. We decided to set our packs down and see if we could find some type of trail. It is quite common that animals would find or make pathways through this kind of brush, and we often used their trails while hiking. After searching for a trail for awhile and not finding any, we decided to just head into the bushes. Many, perhaps even most of the bushes were fifteen to twenty feet tall. They had so many branches that we found it easier to actually walk from branch to branch and not set foot on the ground.

The farther we ventured into this Manzanita forest, the stranger it felt. We had travelled quite a distance and all that we could see were branches. There was no view to look out over, just more branches. We stopped and looked around, there were only more bushes and more branches. We thought we had probably travelled at least a mile through this maze, and we suddenly realized that there were no landmarks, no paths, no view outside of these bushes. We wondered how easy it would be to find our way back out! Since we had been walking, climbing over branches, there were no marks on the ground showing we had come from a particular direction. As we turned around and attempted to head back from what we believed was the direction we had come from, it was obvious that these bushes were going to keep our original path a secret that only they would know.

I could tell that my brother was getting a little worried about being lost in this Manzanita jungle. I decided it was time to start telling jokes. I told one and we both laughed, then he shared one and this continued for awhile with both of us having a great time. Here we were, somewhat lost and still having one of those shared times that you never forget. With both of us laughing and focused on telling jokes, I have no idea how long it took us to find our way out, but suddenly we popped out of the bushes so close to where we had entered that we could see our packs laying on the ground right where we had left them.

We decided that it was getting too late to look for a better spot, so we set up camp right there on the mountainside. I had always set up camp at a creek so we would have water, but it was only going to be for one night. We noticed that clouds had been building and it was looking and feeling like rain was coming. We set up the tent and started collecting firewood and also some flat stones that we could set like a little porch just outside the tent where we could take off our boots and keep them out of the dirt.

I heard my brother yell for me and went to see what was up. He had lifted up a flat rock to bring to camp and found a huge scorpion under it. This was not only the biggest scorpion that I had ever seen, but it was an olive green color. I had not even heard of a green scorpion before. After checking him out for a couple of minutes, we carefully put the same flat stone back over him. Live and let live. We both felt that it was almost an honor to be able to see this little guy in all of his green glory.

Just as we were finishing setting up camp, it started to rain, not sprinkle, but rain like you get up in the mountains. It was still very light outside and I really didn't want to be holed up in the tent all evening and night, but what choice was there? We had brought some playing cards and bags of cookies. We decided to pass the time with some cookie poker. It was a blast. We laughed and were having such a good time, all the while the rain continued and even came down harder. Then we realized that water was starting to intrude into the tent. It was coming from the bottom, and I needed to get outside to see what I could do to stop it. We had not counted on it raining and did not have rain gear. So I took off all my clothes and went out into the storm naked.

Since we had set up the tent on the side of a mountain, rain water was washing down the mountain side like a river. We had brought a small shovel to use to put our fires out. I grabbed it, and in the middle of the storm I dug a trench from the high side of the tent around both sides, diverting the water away and leaving the tent safe from its onslaught. Even though it was storming, it really wasn't that cold outside, and being out there naked on the side of a mountain in the pouring rain, was another one of those experiences that I'll never forget.

In the morning, we packed up camp and headed back down to the creek. We headed up the creek and camped overnight and the next day headed back to the car. We crossed the creek in the same place we had two days earlier, rock hopping our way to the other side. It was a short trip, but we had both had such a great time. I had often done cool things with my little brother and I tried to include him in many of my activities, but this trip was a game changer. I saw that he could keep up with me and that the two of us together could have a great time.

As we got back to the car and began to put our things in the trunk, I suddenly realized that my knife was missing! We looked everywhere, in the packs, around the car, in my laundry bag, but no knife. I back tracked for about a half mile and knew that it was futile. The knife was gone and I had no idea where it might be. Even if I back tracked all the way to our last camp, there was little chance that I would be able to find it. Heartbroken, I headed back to the car. As we drove off, I was so sad about the knife and yet so grateful for having such a good time with my brother.

Two years later I was on a backpacking trip with my best friend Dennis. We had planned on hiking to a lake that we had never been to before and spending a few days there. We parked in the same spot where my brother and I had parked two years earlier. Our plan was to hike to the big creek and cross it at the same waterfall, but from there we were heading off in a different direction, following a trail that would take us to much higher country, and to the small lake that we had heard about. We helped each other get our packs on and adjusted, and then we were on our way. Dennis and I had gone through high school together and we had both been on the gymnastics team and had the same group of friends.

We talked about high school and some of the ridiculous things that we had done, laughed as we reminisced about old friends and kept up the conversation as we followed the trail. We reached the creek and found that it was flowing higher and faster than any time we had seen it before. Rock hopping across the big boulders was going to be a little scary. Dennis went first and made it across without incident. He was an amazing athlete and made it look easy. I started to cross with much more care than he had seemed to put into it. Rock hopping was one thing, but doing it with a fifty pound backpack on was quite another matter. As I would launch from one rock and land on another, the pack would shift a little and make it difficult to catch my balance. I made it about two thirds of the way across and was perched atop a rock that was pretty round and probably about five feet in diameter. I was suddenly struck by the strangest feeling. I looked around and although everything looked like it should, something was screaming inside me to pay attention.

I stood there for a minute or two trying to understand what was going on. I finally made my way to the other side of the creek where Dennis was waiting for me and wondering what the heck I was doing. I took my backpack off and headed back to the rock in the middle of the creek. The sound of the waterfall was intense and I was totally aware of the dangerous position I was in. I knelt down on the rock and tried looking into the creek, trying to see the bottom. It was probably two and half to three foot deep, but the water was moving so fast, that I could not see the bottom. As I knelt there on the rock, I somehow knew that what was calling me, was my father's knife. I couldn't see it, and yet I knew that it was there. I sat down and took my boots off, then the rest of my clothes. The water was rushing by so fast and I knew that it was most likely just below freezing. The only thing keeping the water from turning to ice was the speed that it was travelling. I tried laying on the rock and reaching as far into the water as I could, but I couldn't feel the bottom. Dennis was watching the whole thing and had no idea what I was doing. I couldn't tell him because the waterfall was too loud. I reluctantly slid my feet into the creek and found the water felt even colder than I expected. I lowered myself down until I was standing on the rocky bottom, still holding onto the boulder to keep from being washed down the waterfall. The water was about two and half feet deep next to the rock and I reached down with my right hand searching for the knife.

I don't know how I knew the knife was there. There was no way of seeing it from any position, but I reached under to where the round boulder was resting on the creek bottom and felt the handle of the knife. I pulled it out of the water and was overwhelmed with gratitude. I hopped back onto the boulder, grabbed my clothes and crossed over to the bank. There are no words that can describe the joy of being reunited with this metal and bone object. There are no words that I know of to share that could explain the mystery of how I was called to find this treasure. There was such an inner knowing of what I was doing and at the same time a confusion in my mind that was saying that it just didn't make sense. One part of me knew exactly where the knife was, and the rest of me had no understanding of what I was doing. Yet it happened just the way I described, a mystical moment that defies logic and begs for a deeper understanding of reality.

I still have the knife, the two years it spent in the river left some small pits and some staining on it, only adding to its amazing character. This was a story that has helped me question the true workings of life. I have often thought to myself that a mystical event is something that should not be possible if life is what we are led to believe. If even one event happens that is outside of the rules of reality, then it has to mean we need a much bigger view of what is real. At the very least we need to have an open mind, so the question is, how open? If our minds are open, then what are the possibilities?

Story #7-Who are you in the Void

I had been doing daily meditations for years and had been using the technique that I described earlier of descending the stairs along the rock cliffs, through the archway and onto my beach. So many wonderful understandings had been shared with me in this magical place. One beautiful morning while I was feeling quite open and peaceful, I once again sat on my couch and journeyed down the stairs to my most private space.

So here I am, on a beach created in my mind, communicating with my guide. Never have I asked him if he had a name, because it just never seemed to make sense to ask myself if I had a name. I soon found that most of the time when I would reach out to my guide, it was to ask questions. After years of asking specific questions regarding events going on in my life or questions about how life works, I reached a place where I realized that this guide had more information than my little conscious mind could ever hope to have. I decided to let my guide determine the direction of our communications. I would sit back and relax and simply ask, "What is it that I most need to know right now?" I would not have a clue as to where he was going to take me, and that made things so much more interesting.

As I sat and reached out, or perhaps reached inward to ask my question," What is it that I most need to know right now?" I felt his presence right away, and to my surprise, I was whisked out of my body, through the roof of the house and out into space! It all happened so fast, but there I was out in the darkness of space. I looked around, and was surprised to see nothing. There were no stars, no Earth, just open space. It is difficult to describe the feeling of floating in an infinite void. I had what seemed to be a body, but with nothing to compare to, there was no way of knowing if my body was tiny, or if it took up most of the infinite space. I felt quite comfortable floating peacefully and not feeling that I needed anything. Suddenly, I was aware of my guide's presence and he asked me, "Who Are You?" I thought about it and began by identifying myself as a husband, a contractor, a son, a brother, but then he interrupted my descriptions with another question. He said, "All that is true on Earth, but who are you here?"

I looked around again and literally let out a gasp! Without something to be in relationship with, how could I have a description and who could I be? It was actually frightening to no longer be all the things that I believed made me the being that I thought I was. Without something outside of myself, of what importance could I be? It was totally amazing to go from floating peacefully in the void to now being frightened at not having an identity. Everything that I thought made me the person that I knew myself to be, no longer applied here. In fact I could find no description of myself other than to say that I was somehow aware. There was a knowingness that I simply was. My guide only left me there a short time, and then he turned me around to where I was looking down on the Earth. What a relief, I could be somebody again!

Somehow, from this vantage point, looking down on Earth, I could see everything going on! I could see babies being born, people dying, lovers making love, people lashing out in anger. I could see people waging war and treating each other with such hostility. I could see the acts of kindness and compassion. I could see the ecosystem with trees, plants, animals and even the bacteria. It felt like anything that could possibly happen, was all actually happening. From this point of view, I felt no judgment about any of it. In fact, what I felt was just an amazing amount of gratitude! We as human beings have been given the gift of contrast!

I had an experience of being in nothingness, and then I was shown everythingness. I know that is an exaggeration, but at the time it felt like all possibilities were being explored, the good, the bad, the joy, the sorrow, sickness, vitality, loss and gain. We were given the opportunity to experience contrast and have a point of view about it. It may sound strange that someone could feel gratitude about the suffering taking place on planet earth, but there was an understanding that in the totality of things, suffering launches us into greater states of being.

Over the years, I have shared my experience of this meditation with a number of friends. I had found it to be one of the most transformative meditations that I have ever had. In times of turmoil or suffering, I would remember being in gratitude for everything happening on earth and I would look at my suffering to see what gift might be hidden inside of it. Later I also began to see that the short time I had spent in the void was an invitation. It had all happened so fast, and seeing the earth again, putting all my attention back on it because it was familiar, while it had seemed that the void was lacking everything. Years later, it almost felt like the void was calling me. I remembered in the meditation, I had been floating so peacefully in the void, and it hadn't been until my guide asked me who I was that I suddenly felt the fear of not having my familiar surroundings. In fact upon reflection, the peace was so profound that I actually felt whole. There was nothing missing and yet there was nothing there ether.

This meditation had shown me the dichotomy of points of view. I could be floating in the void and feel that I was totally fulfilled and whole, or I could be floating in nothingness and feel that I lacked everything. I could look at the earth and all the objects that I perceived and be in gratitude for there being something outside of myself to be in relationship with, or I could look at the earth and all the objects and suffering and feel myself as so insignificant and alone, and see life as such a struggle.

Which point of view is correct? What makes us choose one point of view over another? Can both views be true and accurate? If there is the opportunity to choose which point of view we are going to embrace, why would we ever choose one that includes suffering, separateness, struggle and turmoil? Is it even possible in this physical plane of existence to know the whole truth of anything, or is a point of view all we are capable of?

When I had first experienced this meditation, I believed that the sole purpose of it had been for me to appreciate the earth and be in gratitude for the contrast of experiences available here, but now I believe that perhaps my short time in the void had planted a seed of a greater reality that would slowly take root and take apart my very limited understanding of who I really am. Now I often go back to floating in that same void in my meditations and sometimes even while I am awake and taking a break from my thoughts.

Some people describe the void as blackness, but my experience is that even though there is not light the way that we think of it, nor are there objects for any light to reflect off of, there is not an absence of light either. If an object were to suddenly appear in the void, it would easily and clearly be seen. The void is a common term used in New Age and metaphysical circles. Is the void a place? Is the void a state of mind or a state of being? Is the void the absence of everything, or the garden from which everything is born?

As I once again sat in meditation, I found myself in the void. The first time my guide had brought me to this experience, I was floating in a vastness with no way of knowing if I was a tiny speck in the void, or I could have been larger than the largest of galaxies. With nothing to be compared with, size seemed meaningless. This time however, I knew that I had no body and therefore no limits. I was the void, being infinite and whole. There was no sense of needing anything. There was knowing of self and a sweet sense of total peace. The knowing of self wasn't a knowing of a limited personality, but a knowing of an unlimited, contented awareness of being. Thoughts were unnecessary, and in fact a single thought, made up of words, would immediately put an end to the infinite peace.

Words are descriptions, and always imply duality. There is this and then there is that other thing. There is self and then something else that is outside of self, whether that other thing is an object, an idea, or a memory, as long as words are used even in thought, duality is implied. In the void without a body and without words, duality does not exist, there is only awareness. As I use the word "awareness" I use it to describe the indescribable. To use the words peace, joy, love, wholeness all pale in comparison to the actual experience. Awareness is not a place nor is it a state of being. Awareness does not take place in time or space. In fact it is more like time and space take place in awareness.

Having a separate self or sensing that we are a separate entity is in a way just an illusion. This illusion is seen or experienced through a "point of view" and never through the wholeness of that which we truly are.

Story #8-A Chance to Stay

In 1980 I was working for a restaurant chain in the San Francisco Bay Area. I had been tasked with the job of turning a couple of existing restaurants in the Reno, Nevada area into our name restaurants. I had been a district manager for a couple of years and was the "go to guy" for trouble shooting problems and getting restaurants back on track. This new adventure seemed quite up my alley and I had been looking forward to the challenge.

I had purchased a house in the East Bay and lived there with my girlfriend Trish, my younger brother Jim and my mother Dolores. The house was in a housing track with each home looking very similar to the next, but it was the first home that I had ever been able to purchase. It was a beautiful summer day as I pulled away from the driveway and started my five hour drive to Reno. I had only been on the road about an hour, when I started feeling a strange call to go back home. This was long before cell phones and I decided to ignore the feeling and continue my drive. I passed through a number of cities, and it seemed the farther I drove the stronger the feeling to go home became.

Driving up highway 80 going over Donner Pass, I decided to stop and call home. I pulled into a gas station and used the pay phone. I talked with my mother who assured me that everything was fine, nothing was going on out of the ordinary. Relieved, I got back in the car and headed onto the highway. To my dismay, the feeling to return home did not go away, instead it seemed even more intense. Reno was not far and so I kept going. Finally I reached my destination, the first restaurant where I was to begin my work. The manager was expecting me and greeted me in the parking lot. We sat outside going over plans, and as I listened to him, half of my attention was still on the calling to go home. It was difficult to focus on the business in front of me, but I was there to complete a job, and I was determined to do it to the best of my abilities.

My father had always taken pride in what ever work he was doing. He had mostly been a salesman. He had sold Kirby vacuum cleaners, worked at numerous car lots and for a time even worked at a Piper dealer selling single and twin-engine airplanes. For him, it did not matter what he was selling or where he was working, it was always of utmost importance to do it to the best of his abilities. He was quite forceful in his demands that I have this same work ethic. To this day, I am grateful for his determination that I learn this lesson, yet now I also see the baggage that came with that lesson.

There was so much to get done in a short period of time, getting this restaurant converted. There was the layout of the kitchen and dining area, training the manager and employees, setting up the food suppliers and other vendors. Getting the advertising arranged, along with menus, menu boards and signage. The amount of work kept my attention on what needed to be accomplished, but at periods throughout the day, I would be aware of the deep calling to return home. As I would return each night to my hotel room, I would be swept up in the urge or desire to go home.

Each morning, it was back to work, and each evening was the reminder that I needed to go home. I pondered over why this was happening. Was someone in some type of trouble at home and they just didn't want to worry me? I had no idea if this was a warning of some difficulty that was ready to play-out, or if it was some type of welcomed event that I might miss if I didn't get my butt home.

The days in Reno went along smoothly and after several weeks, it was time for me to finally head home! Yeah! My last day was a long one, but I wanted to get everything finished so I could leave that afternoon. I was exhausted but also excited as I drove off. The urge to go home was the strongest that I had felt so far. As I drove, I pondered about the restaurants that I was leaving. Did I forget anything, had I trained everyone well enough? Had I accomplished what I needed to?

I had reached Donner Summit again and was heading down the mountain feeling both mentally and physically drained. It was around 5:00 PM, a beautiful evening and traffic was fairly light. I was so intent on getting home as soon as I could, that I really didn't realize how tired I was. As I was travelling at a speed of around 65mph, I fell asleep! I was off in the never never land of unconsciousness when I was awakened by the sound of a horn. I opened my eyes to the sight of the concrete barriers that separate the directions of traffic. I was heading directly into the barrier! To this day, I cannot understand how I was able to turn, not lose control and miss the barrier. In such a short time, I had fallen asleep, someone noticed that I was asleep, they had time to react by honking their horn and I somehow had time to miss the concrete barrier!

I never saw the car or the person that had honked and brought me back from my sleep. I pulled off the highway and found a safer place to sleep. That's a joke, because just about any place is safer to sleep than behind the wheel on a highway. After about an hour and a half of a great nap, I pulled back onto the highway and was headed home again. After a short time, maybe a half hour of driving, I somehow began to realize that the home where I had lived for the last few years and the home that I was heading for now was not the home that I was being called to go to. I was so confused. Where was it that I was supposed to be going? I thought about my house and family waiting for me and the more that I thought about them, the more I knew that I was not going to the home that had been calling me.

When I reached my house and walked inside, I felt so out of place, almost like a stranger. It was like I was living someone else's life. I was in a house that I knew, but I was not supposed to be there. It was great seeing Trish and greeting my mother and brother, but that did not stop the most uncomfortable feeling of being in the wrong place. After a good night sleep, I woke up feeling every bit as out of place as I had felt when I had first arrived.

After weeks of working in Reno, I had the next several days off. Everyone at home was happy to have me back, the house seemed as though nothing was out of the ordinary, but I was different. I was out of place. Being able to hold Trish again was wonderful. We had always enjoyed an amazing relationship. I can't remember a time where we were not getting along. We never really argued. We were able to talk about anything and everything. There were no secrets kept from each other. While I was still in Reno, I had talked with her about this crazy feeling of needing to return home. Although this particular experience was different than any other that I had gone through, I had many other "mystical" type experiences in the past. Trish was supportive and believed that this all meant something and that it would become clear soon.

I had been meditating daily for several years and it occurred to me that perhaps I might find an answer at a deeper level.

Normally I would sit on the couch or the floor while meditating, but for some reason I felt that this meditation needed to be different. I decided to lay flat on my bed and I asked Trish to not only stay with me, but I asked her to put her hand on my heart during the meditation. I believed that this experience was going to be different and I wanted to know if my heart slowed down or if it beat faster while I was in deep meditation. I had never asked for anyone to touch me in any way before and was unsure if having her hand on me would keep me from going deep.

As I lay on the bed I got as comfortable as I could. Trish got into a position that she believed she could maintain for the duration of the meditation. She put her hand over my heart. I started by taking several deep calming breaths. As my body relaxed, I began to put my attention on an area just above and behind my heart. My breathing began to slow and my body relaxed even more. Several times there seemed to be a "jolt" that felt like my body would jump, something similar to what you might feel as you fall asleep and suddenly pop-up awake. Then I would feel my body relax again and go even deeper. As I felt myself letting go of all concerns and falling into a wonderful state of peace, I asked "where is home?"

I allowed only this single thought to occupy my mind. I would slowly repeat, "where is home?" With this single focus, my body disappeared, and I felt a cloud surround me. It seemed that perhaps I might have a face, but there was no recognition of a body or even a head. I believe that I still had the sensation of having/being a face, and this face was totally encompassed by a beautiful cloud. I again thought about "where is home," and felt as though I was light as air. I felt like I was floating up and going home! There are no words to describe the joy, peace and excitement of going home. I floated up as if carried by this wonderful cloud. I could sense that this home was welcoming me and that those that loved me so deeply were waiting. I seemed to recognize three souls that I was floating towards. Their arms were stretching towards me, waiting to grasp me and welcome me. Although I did not know these souls in this lifetime, I understood that I was deeply connected to them and loved by them with a level of emotion that I had not known in this life. Then I felt that I was slowly being pushed back down, as if a puff of wind had blown down on me. Then again I was floating up with such joy! Then again a slight pull back down. I don't know how many times I went up and back down, but eventually I believe that I lost all sensation.

As I awoke from my meditation, I found that Trish had climbed completely on top me! During the meditation, I had totally forgotten about her. I had not even noticed her hand on my chest. The only sensation that I could remember was that of floating and then of being lightly pushed down. I knew that I had gone deeper in this meditation than any that I had ever done before, but how could I not feel someone climbing on top of me!

As I looked at her, I could see that she was scared. She was white and almost frantic. I asked her what was wrong and she began to cry. I slowly sat up and hugged her, trying to calm her. I could feel her shaking, so I just held her for awhile. "Honey are you okay?" I asked. She pulled back a little to look at me, still shaking she began to explain that while her hand was on my chest, my body began to float off of the bed! She pushed it back onto the bed, but it started to float up again and again she pushed it back down. Each time my body started to float, it took more pressure for Trish to push it back down. Finally out of panic and fear, she climbed on top of me. She stayed there holding my body down until I woke up from the meditation.

This took place 40 years ago, but to this day Trish swears that it happened just as I have written it. From my point of view, it was all quite light and wonderful, except that I did not get to see the home that I was floating off to. I don't know if my body was actually floating, or if what Trish was feeling or sensing was some type of energy, but in her reality, she believes that she saved my life that day. As for me, after that meditation, the desire or urge to go home went away. I have never had that feeling again. Out of curiosity, I have tried a handful of times to repeat the steps of meditation, focus, asking where is home, and nothing has worked. I believe without that intense urge, the door is closed.

It was sometime later that in telling this story, I suddenly understood that the drive back from Reno was a possible "exit point" for me. There was a real possibility for me to hit that concrete divider and not survive. I never saw the car or person that honked and caused me to wake up in time to miss the divider. I can still picture heading into that concrete wall and I honestly don't understand how I avoided hitting it. I wonder who it was that saved my life that day. I wonder if they know what a gift they gave me, a chance to live for decades longer. A chance to be with my family again, and a chance that allowed me to meet a wonderful woman and get married. For whatever reason, I did not go "home" that day, at least not to the home that had been calling me.

The more I thought about my life and what all has transpired since that drive back from Reno, the more gratitude I have for the amazing gift of life. There are many times that it appears that we go through our daily lives and not much changes. We get up each morning, go to work, come home, spend time with family and then repeat it again and again. Yet as I look back over the past forty years, so much has changed. In fact, looking back over such a long period it seems that nothing stayed the same. As a contractor, I have met so many people, worked on so many projects, learned so many things, made so many new friends and have been so many places. I met Anna, who was already the mother of 2 wonderful young children. We had lots of adventures together. We experienced so many joys with the kids. I learned much more about love relationships, but we finally parted ways.

I had several girlfriends after my marriage ended, but one day I met Cristina. Over the next several weeks, I found myself having one mystical experience after another. Many of them were directly related to Cristina, but somehow it was as if a door had opened and I would never be the same again. We ended up getting together and she moved to California to be with me. She was a "healer," doing body work but also some profound work of the Spirit too. Together, I feel that we impacted many lives in many ways.

It has been said that a butterfly flapping its wings in Africa affects everyone on the planet[i]. As I look back over the forty years, I can see the ripple effect of my life! I see and believe that because I did not die on the trip back from Reno, my being here has affected the entire planet. The people that I influenced and then the people they influenced and so on and so on. It now makes sense that we all change the world in many ways. What may seem like an ordinary life can and does affect everyone. In fact, if it is true that my life has affected everyone on the planet, it also means that every person born as long as planet Earth exists is also affected by my life, even long after I'm gone.

I truly believe that every choice we make changes the world! Whether we smile at another driver or "flip them off," we create a ripple. If we hand some change to someone in need or just offer encouraging words, we create a ripple. Without realizing it, we are constantly creating these ripples and we have no idea how far they are travelling. We are ripple machines, running into other ripple makers all the time and not knowing it. When we are on the phone and on hold waiting for our turn to get help with a question, we are being rippled by those ahead of us. When we are in line at a drive through, we are rippling those behind us and we don't even know it. When we ask a question in class, we are rippling again.

I live in the foothills of the Sierras in California. My mailbox is more than half a mile up a dirt road and is one in a bank of mailboxes. It is common to meet one of my neighbors while getting my mail. A couple of days ago, I met one of them at the mailbox, she had lost her husband a little over a year ago. We chatted for about twenty minutes and I was telling her about writing this very story, and about the ripples. We finished our chat and each drove away. As I pondered our visit, I understood that the rest of her day was now changed. She was now twenty minutes later for everything that would come the rest of the day. She also now had my story to think about and possibly share. Our twenty minute talk had changed her day and that also meant it changed the rest of her life and mine too. As I had shared my story and explained the ripples, we were busy making those very ripples.

As I ponder my rippling power, I have to ask myself, "What do I want to ripple out to the world?" Do I want to ripple Joy? Do I want to create Love ripples? Do I want my ripples to be uplifting or disturbing? Can I send out Peace ripples? Whether I want to or not, I am constantly sending ripples. If I sit quietly in my own house, all by myself, not being in contact with anyone, I believe that I am still rippling the world. It may seem that our lives are not of much consequence in the broader view of world events, but in this understanding, we are in fact world changers! We cannot help but alter the world with our experience of it. How important am I, if everything I do changes everyone? Every decision I make is going to change everything, so can I choose to make changes that bring more beauty and joy to the world? By knowing my rippling power, can I make better choices for myself and for everyone? What would happen if groups got together for the purpose of rippling joy or peace?

I am aware that experiments have been done with groups getting together to meditate or to heal. These experiments have shown the ability to alter crime levels in cities, help with individual healings and generally increase the level of wellbeing. If we can only ripple the level of consciousness that we are vibrating at, then perhaps the single most important mission we can ever undertake is to make it our priority to be the kindest, most loving, happiest person that we can be. This is being a "Super Hero!" This is how reality is created.

Story #9-Orly

I was in my early forties and had just finished going through a difficult divorce. I still loved my former wife and was having a rough time. In fact, for the first time in my life I felt as though I needed some real help. I just did not seem to be able to cope with the loss and how different my life was without her. We had spent most our time together, even working together in my contracting business. We would go to the store together, go for bike rides or hiking up in the hills nearby where we lived. When we had married, she had shared custody of her two young children, a son and a daughter. I loved the kids as if they were my own, but along with losing my wife, who was quite angry with me, I also lost the children.

Although I had support from my parents, my brother, my sister and some friends, they all just wanted to tell me what a terrible person my ex-wife was and that I was better off without her. They believed that she was the cause of all our problems. This was not what I wanted to hear. I knew that she was an amazing woman and that I was just as responsible for the break-up as she was. It just was not in me to demonize her to make myself feel better.

One morning while I was reading the newspaper, I saw an ad for a "Divorce Recovery Workshop." It was starting in a few days and was not far from where I lived. I called that day and signed up for a spot. Little did I know how that workshop would change my life! The universe is always sending curve balls; when one door closes another opens, often in ways that you would not imagine.

Since my wife had first moved out, I had been quite distraught. I had trouble concentrating on my contracting business and had not been eating very well. In a matter of a few weeks, I had lost close to twenty pounds and felt much of my physical strength had vanished along with the weight. I was really looking forward to the workshop and hoped that it would get me back into a happier frame of being.

As I walked into the large room where the workshop was to take place, I was surprised to see that there were many more women than men and most seemed to be around my age. I was excited to be able to talk with people that were going through the same challenges that I was dealing with. I believe that there were around sixty to seventy people taking the class.

The instructor was a man in his mid-forties, kind and compassionate. It was obvious that he had led other such classes and seemed quite confident. The first part of each class consisted of the instructor lecturing on emotions, relationships and expectations. One of the key points that seemed to resonate with me was that many of us have been in some type of love relationship since high school. I know that in my case, there was hardly a time when I was not in a relationship with a steady girlfriend all the way up until I had married at thirty two years old. The instructor talked about how in cases like mine, there just was never a long enough period of being alone to really get to know yourself. Without a strong sense of self, who would we be bringing into another relationship? I had never thought about such a thing, yet it really struck me as true. As soon as one relationship would end, I would look for someone else to fill the void. I was not seeing or feeling myself to be whole without a partner. What if I could be whole by myself? If I felt whole on my own, then I could bring a "whole" person into a new relationship. Just this one realization was enough for me to begin the healing process and have some acceptance that it was ok to be alone for awhile.

The second part of each class consisted of breaking us up into groups of six to eight people. We were given instructions on topics to share, from the types of challenges that our marriages had endured, to how we might do things or see things in a different way, and taking responsibility for what happens. I found these group talks very helpful and enlightening. It was nice to hear how other men had behaved in their marriages, but it was really helpful to hear what the women had to share.

One thing that became quite evident in the very first class was that many of my classmates were looking for another partner. It had not occurred to me that this would be a great place to meet single women, but here they were, all to ready to jump back into another relationship. Several seemed very interested in me, and I can't deny that I was somewhat interested in getting to know a couple of them. Still, I was really taken with the thought of taking time to be ok with being alone and seeing myself as "whole."

The classes were held just once a week and I found myself looking forward to each one. From the very first class, I could feel myself relaxing and my emotional body healing. I believe that it was during the third class when we broke into our smaller groups and began sharing our thoughts that it fell on this particular woman named Orly to speak. As she shared her story it was amazing that she seemed to have no anger, no hurt and no polarity about her divorce. It was evident that she still felt love for her ex-husband and yet was quite ok with what happened. It was as if she was feeling herself as complete and whole with or without a partner. I felt myself being drawn to understand her better. I was being pulled to her, but not in a romantic way. Even though she was quite pretty and obviously single, the attraction that I was feeling towards her had little to do with male, female roles.

As the class was ending for the evening, I had the opportunity to meet her. I walked up and introduced myself and said, "I am not sure why, but I need to know you." I have to say that this seemed like a very strange line to say to a woman, but she looked at me as though she totally understood what I meant. It was almost 10:00 PM, but she said that she had not had dinner, and that I was welcome to join her. We got to our cars and I followed her to a nearby restaurant.

After getting seated at our table, we began to talk about the class and the things going on in both of our lives. Orly shared with me that she had signed up for the class by mistake. She thought that she had signed up for a totally different type of class, but she also believed that nothing happens that is not supposed to, so she decided to attend the class. Looking back at it now, perhaps she had been sent there to change my life, because after the next eight hours, my life would not be the same.

Orly explained that Anna, my ex-wife and I had shared many lifetimes together and although my love for her was deep and genuine, I had other things that I was to do with this lifetime, and I would avoid doing them as long as we were together. Anna was the one that had left me, and I should be quite grateful to her because I did not have the strength to move forward myself. Orly's words resonated with such clarity that I almost instantly began to feel relief over our divorce. The belief that both our marriage and our divorce had all taken place just as it was supposed to and that I was on the right path, allowed me to experience a sense of ease and comfort that I had not felt in quite some time.

As we left the restaurant we walked together to her car and I stood by as she opened the trunk. There were boxes of papers, many were drawings and many had writing in a language that I did not recognize. She reached for a small stack of papers that had both drawings and this strange language. She pulled out a single sheet and handed it to me. This particular paper had a drawing of a person with what I would describe as a vortex above its head. Below the drawing was some of this language that somehow looked familiar and yet like nothing that I had ever seen before. Orly instructed me to study this paper before getting into bed for the night and then place it on the night stand next to the bed.

I had never met anyone like this lovely lady and there simply are no words to describe the peace and confidence that she radiated. We each got in our vehicles and I drove home pondering how the night had gone, from the class, to meeting Orly, to the restaurant, her insights into my relationship with my ex-wife, whom I still hold nothing but love for even today, and now this unusual drawing and instructions.

It was pretty late by the time I got home, so I immediately got myself ready for bed. My mind was still a whirlwind, but I was so tired I thought I would be able to go right to sleep. I sat on the edge of the bed and looked at the paper. I did not understand any of the words and so I spent a few minutes mostly studying the drawing, then I placed the paper on the nightstand and crawled into bed.

Almost as soon as my head hit the pillow I began to get a strange sensation. I had never experienced anything like it before, but it felt as though information was pouring into my head from somewhere up and out in the universe. It was as if my brain was a computer and information was being downloaded into it. It seemed to be a massive amount of information and was rushing in so fast that I did not have time to grasp it. Parts of it I saw as images but most of it just felt like information or knowledge that I somehow knew would be made clear to me later. My brain seemed to be on overload as it would try to focus on pieces of information flying by.

After about an hour of lying in bed and this onslaught of information pouring in, I realized that I was not going to sleep anytime soon, nor did I want to sleep. I got out of bed and made my way to the living room and a cozy spot on the couch. There I sat for hours as the download continued. I had a smile on my face as big as any smile I had ever had. Although I had gone to bed exhausted, the thrill of what was happening had wiped away any lack of energy. Every once in awhile I would grasp a piece of information and I was beginning to understand what it was all about.

I was shown that there was a project that I could/should work on. I was shown how this project would make an impact on so many people around the world, perhaps enough to start a movement that would change the views of millions. I was shown how this project would make enough money to fund the next project that was going to cost an incredible amount. This second project was not going to make money, but it was going to be an opportunity for the world to reach out for peace in a way that it had never experienced before. As I saw and understood what I was being shown, I sat there on my couch repeating the words "Oh My God," "Oh My God."

There really is no way to describe the feelings that were flowing through me. Joy at seeing how a more peaceful Earth was possible, seeing how many lives would not be wasted in war, and how this would be possible because of people choosing peace instead of violence. At the same time, I am saying to myself that I am just one person and the whole thing seemed overwhelming.

I was shown how my life would go if I were to move forward with these amazing projects, and I have to say that it all looked fantastic! There would be so many challenges and yet so much joy. There would be so many people that would step in to help and choose to take part in both projects. Then I was shown how I could choose to stay being a contractor and what that life would look like. It was a good life, quite normal with friends and family and years of work followed by retirement. I felt no pressure to choose one life over the other, instead there was simply an invitation to live an extraordinary life.

At the time, I could see no reason for choosing the path of being a contractor and passing up such an amazing opportunity. There was no doubt that I would choose the path that would make me live a larger life, a life so different than I could have imagined, a life that would challenge me to go outside of the "Box" of how I had seen myself living. Each step would be like nothing I had ever done before. The people that I would meet would be life changing. How could I possibly pass up such an amazing chance?

As the sun came up, the living room began to fill with the light of a new day. I was still sitting on the couch with this silly smile and processing the information that I had been given, it felt like I understood only about ten percent of the information and that the remainder would filter into understanding as I needed it.

It is hard to believe or grasp how my life view had changed in the last twenty four hours. The morning before I had been sitting on this same couch filled with the loss of my marriage. I had been looking forward to the workshop that evening and hoping that it would ease some of my suffering. Now I was sitting in the same spot and seeing the world like I never would have imagined. I felt ready to change my life and head out on a new path.

Orly and I became good friends. I helped her once in awhile on projects that she was working on and introduced her to some of my amazing friends. We had many discussions about life and reality, but none compared to the one that changed my life, the conversation in the restaurant about how it was not "meant to be" for my wife and I to remain together, the drawing and the strange language, the information download and the hope for a new life.

As I am writing about that evening, some twenty years have gone by, I am somewhat sorry to say that I have only in the past couple of weeks retired from being a contractor. Although I have been on a journey of discovery, I did not choose to pursue the projects that I had been offered. It is all too easy to blame my sense of responsibility that I felt towards my crew and my family to maintain an income and provide for their welfare. It seemed at the time that it would be selfish of me to suddenly shut down my contracting company and go off in a direction that may not provide any income for the foreseeable future. Then as the days passed, life and work once again directed my choices.

I would also like to share that as I was writing this story, I realized that no one has begun this first project that I had been offered. My mind exploded with thoughts and my body responded with emotions, "Am I still supposed to move forward with it?" It feels like I am right back on the couch and the information has just been downloaded. I thought that I knew exactly what I was going to do with my retirement time, but now all that is up in the air. I now feel compelled to finish this collection of stories quickly and prepare for what is to come.

Story #10-What's Important

It was early morning, the house was perfectly quiet and I was very much awake. It had all the ingredients for a great time to meditate. I sat on the couch and dropped into a wonderfully peaceful state. As I reached the place where I felt that I could let go of everything and simply expand into infiniteness, I noticed that my guide was present. Feeling so light and joyful, I asked him, "What is it that I most need to know right now"?

I suddenly found myself in a beautiful meadow. There were trees scattered about that grew denser as they got closer to a wonderful creek that meandered near-by. It was a sunny day and the area seemed to be filled with life. Birds flying with a backdrop of the amazingly blue cloudless sky, deer quietly grazing on the green meadow grasses. I could see a couple of squirrels chasing each other through the branches of a nearby tree. This place seemed to be peace manifested.

I could feel my guide was present, and he somehow made me aware that I was the only human left on Earth! In some strange way, I was able to scan the entire earth searching for other humans but could find none. I understood that I was indeed the last man standing. I could sense that the human race had been gone from this planet for quite some time, yet here I was in this place of peace. My guide then asked me, "What are you going to do with your life? What's important?"

For some reason, I was not afraid of being the only human here. I looked around and pondered his questions. This place was amazing and it seemed to be asking to be explored. I could see that many of the trees were bearing fruit, and I understood that finding food and surviving would not be very difficult. I responded to his questions, saying that I would spend my life exploring as much of this wonderful planet as I possibly could and that what seemed important, was to learn or understand how I fit into this environment. What types of relationships could I have with the creatures, the plants and even the planet? I wanted to find out if I was just one of billions of creatures living here, or was there a purpose, a special reason for my life, and for living that life here. I understood that I could have a wonderful life here. There was much more to see and discover than I could possibly fit into just one lifetime. I was excited to see how I could fit in with the animals and the environment. I knew that I could live a full and happy life here.

As I was finishing explaining what my life might look like, my guide whisked us off to another place and another time.

Now I was standing on a small round hill, looking down on a cozy little village. Each of the shelters stood alone, with plenty of space dividing them from each other. I could see dozens of people down below and it looked like everyone was quite busy, as though each person had a task and was set on nothing less than accomplishing that task. The scene reminded me of a "Hobbit" village, and the energy in the air felt so welcoming.

Then, my guide repeated his questions, "What are you going to do with your life? What's important?" I looked back down at the village and almost couldn't wait to get down there and be part of this lovely community. Being a General Contractor, and seeing the type of structures in the village, I knew that my skills would be quite appreciated. I explained to my guide that I wanted to join this community, be part of its beautiful energy and contribute everything that I had to offer. Being part of this village seemed to be such a wonderful thing. Friendships and love awaited me here. I could already feel how wonderful it would be to live in such a place and that I could live a full and happy life here.

Again, just as I was finishing explaining what my life might look like, my guide whisked us off to another place and another time.

Now I found myself standing on a sidewalk in what seemed to be a massive city! Hundreds of cars filled the streets in front of me. So many people were crowded on the sidewalks and rushing past me. Unlike the little village I had just left, the energy here was chaotic, the buildings towered above and stood so close together.

I thought about the beautiful meadow that I had started in. There was so much space and peace, and in a way, room for me to be me. I couldn't wait to be part of the life that surrounded me. I thought about the little village and how excited I was to contribute and be welcomed as part of that community. How much room there was for me to be me. How different this huge city felt.

Again, my guide repeated his questions, "What are you going to do with your life? What's important?" I looked around, pondering how I might live in such a place. Although I felt that I could find a way to "fit in" here, I was not sensing that I would be of "value" here. The city seemed to be the same with or without me. Would it be enough to simply live here and survive? How would I experience the uniqueness of being me?

After pondering his questions, I responded by saying that I guess I will need to get an apartment and some furnishings. I'll need a bed a couch a T.V., etc. I'll get a job to earn money to pay for the things that I need. I could see that most of my time would be used in making a "living" so that I might be like everyone else and have the things that everyone else had. I would make friends and in my free time I could "hang out" with them.

It seemed in this reality that my uniqueness was not going to shine through, yet I felt that I could survive here. As large as this city was and in spite of how many people lived here, it felt that there just was not room for the uniqueness that we each vibrate with. There seemed to be expectations of how each of us needed to be. Unlike the previous two lives that I had envisioned, this life seemed "heavy" and limited. Even though I was in the middle of such technology, there was going to be so little time to actually live life.

Suddenly, I am back on my couch, and I could sense that my guide was quite happy with himself, knowing that he had allowed me to actually see what is important. The value in life was not in collecting material objects, nor was it earning money. I am not saying that these things have no importance, but that compared to exploring and building relationships or discovering our own abilities they pale in significance. By relationships, I am referring to not only with other people, but animals, plants, our own bodies and every aspect of this physical world. We are all on a mission to find connections, happiness and love. I don't mean to imply that living in a large city would preclude us from such relationships, but it seemed that with more people there was a greater expectation. It didn't feel like I could just walk outside my apartment and commune with nature. The sounds from the streets flowed through my ears and into my brain almost to the point of competing with my own thoughts. It occurred to me that some people might actually take comfort in this chaos. In some ways with so many other minds around and so many expectations placed on you, life would happen to you without having to make a lot of choices.

We are all unique, experiencing this amazing planet for different reasons. There are an infinite number of ways of expressing ourselves and our talents and abilities. Art, science, technology, politics, clothing, construction, recreation, food, social structure, sports, media, music and religion are just some of the many avenues available to us that allow us to express our own unique styles. Without taking time to understand what we each find important; we are left with the flow of life to make many of our choices for us. What magical opportunities are we missing by not asking ourselves what we truly want out of life? I am not talking about taking five minutes to sit down and ponder such an important subject. I am suggesting that we each take as much time as we need to answer this critical question. For some, the answer may be quite obvious and not much time is needed for contemplation, but for most of us some real soul searching is required.

As I looked back at my life and pondered over what I found to be most important, I was struck by the times that I was truly experiencing joy or love. These times were not while I was on some expensive vacation, or when I closed escrow on the purchase of my first home. They did not include getting drunk with my friends, or even winning awards. The times that seemed to have had the most impact were the times that in a way appeared to be so random, like when I was just a boy and my mother, my sister and I would be listening to a comedian and laughing to the point of rolling on the floor. Or having amazing water balloon fights where my mother would be acting as young and as childish as me and my sister. Taking my little brother on a backpacking trip or sharing some piece of wisdom with him and watching as that information soaked in, knowing that his life was now different because of our time together; made me feel real joy. Remembering baking cookies with my mother seemed to just make me feel warm inside. Taking walks with my wife and holding her hand in mine. These acts of kindness and compassion seemed to take center stage as I looked back at my life. Also, the times that I would let my guard down and allow myself to share my deepest thoughts and feelings with those that seemed like they may benefit in some way from hearing my story.

As great as it might have been at the time, getting that promotion, that raise or that new car, were just minor little blips compared to the things that I really seemed to find value in. It doesn't make sense that I spent ninety percent of my time pursuing the blips and just ten percent on the things that I valued the most. It is said that hindsight is twenty twenty, but that only applies if you take the time to truly examine the past. I also believe that every moment has the potential for us to express and experience joy and love. Both joy and love are ways of vibrating or expressing a level of beingness. Most often we tend to allow whatever is happening outside to control our vibration on the inside. The quest to become a Master is really the quest to become the Master of, or the one that chooses to vibrate love and joy regardless of the circumstances on the outside. What seems to be important is that we have the ability to choose who we want to be moment by moment. We can choose to lose ourselves in despair, fear, anger, guilt or shame; or we can remember that who we truly are is made of light, joy and love. We cannot get lost in love or joy, because that IS who we are. We can only lose ourselves or forget who we are by falling into the pit of the lower vibrations. Perhaps the very emotions of fear or anger are actually just how we perceive the "forgetting" of our true nature.

Story #11-Dimensional Healing[ii]

Part 1-To Believe or not to Believe

In 2001 I was living in the San Francisco Bay Area. I had dated a very interesting lady for a few months and then she accepted a Job in Texas. She was an extraordinary healer and seemed to possess some clairvoyant gifts. After her move to Texas, we would chat on the phone from time to time. The longer she was at her new job, the more she expressed excitement over it. Finally, one day she calls and tells me that the woman she was working for was going to be teaching a class and that I needed to attend.

The class concerned a technique for working on people with cancer. I had been fascinated by things that did not seem to fit with the "laws" of realty that most of us take for granted. I could tell that my ex-girlfriend was profoundly moved by what she was learning, and that she honestly believed that I had to be there and see it for myself. It was thousands of dollars and weeks of time that I did not really have to spare, but for some reason I decided that I would take the class. There was no way that I could possibly know how this class would change my life in so many profound and lasting ways!

I arrived in Texas and was picked up at the airport and driven to a compound in a very small town. There were twelve of us taking the class, and what a diverse group we were. Most everyone had been dedicated to some type of healing practice for years. I was the only one that was a newcomer to doing any type of healing work. Still, because of my interest and passion for anything that was out of the norm, I seemed to fit in with the group. The lady teaching the class was also the owner of the compound. I don't want to use her real name, so I will call her Phoenix. She was a fascinating character, short, dark hair, glasses and moved and talked with such confidence and command. We were all shown our rooms to get settled into. Each room was set up like a dorm, with three to four beds.

On the first day of class, the twelve of us gathered in a very large room sitting in a half circle around Phoenix. A lady came in and sat in a chair next to her. She looked to be in her mid-fifties. Phoenix partially lifted this lady's shirt exposing the side of her left breast. There was a large visible lump on the side of her breast. We watched as Phoenix placed her thumb and index finger on opposite sides of the lump. It looked like she put only slight pressure on the lump, holding it between her thumb and finger. She slowly, gently rolled the lump and kept this gentle movement for a couple of minutes. Phoenix did not make a sound and looked as if she were in meditation. Suddenly she took her hand away and the lump was gone! There was only smooth breast skin visible. We watched as Phoenix looked slightly upward and then coughed forcefully and out of her mouth came the tumor!

I have to say that although I believed that extraordinary things can and do happen, my immediate thought was one of not believing. This had to be a hoax. How could anyone believe for a moment that such a thing is possible? It occurred to me that perhaps I should ask for my money back and head home. Yet it seemed that the others in the class were more accepting that this was truly happening, and they expected such things to be possible. I, however, was not so optimistic.

Part 2-A Dark Secret

For the rest of the day, Phoenix went over how the next several weeks would be laid out. Although I don't want to get into the actual techniques that we were instructed in, I would like to say that during those weeks I witnessed hundreds of events similar to what Phoenix had done on that first day. I can also say with some confidence, that although I never really became adept at these techniques, there were times that I knew I "popped" out some tumors. I would see/feel the tumor in my mind and in a flash of light see it come out and manifest on the ground!

Each day, we would spend about ten hours with our hands on people seeking this help. It was on the second day that I first noticed unusual feelings and thoughts coming to me as I laid my hands on the body in front of me. I would place my hands near a problem area and begin to have thoughts and sense emotions that I knew were not mine. I somehow understood that I was picking up the emotions that were being stored in this part of the body. I was picking up or sensing what the root cause of the cancer was.

I knew or believed that we all hold emotions in different parts of our bodies. Certain stresses we might hold in our neck or shoulders. Fears we might hold in a particular organ. Feelings of not being good enough or feeling unloved would be held somewhere else. It is almost as if these emotions are information stored in cellular memory. Somehow as I laid my hands on these people, I was accessing this stored information. At times when it felt appropriate, I began to talk with these people and share what I was sensing. I remember every one of them telling me that what I was getting was exactly what was going on in their lives.

I found that sensing and sharing these feelings was quite an intimate experience. It was as though I was living their experience. I was feeling their deepest sorrows, their biggest fears, their beliefs in their own unworthiness. Many of these feelings I found difficult to share with the very ones that were living them. One beautiful lady, who lay on a table before me and from all outward appearances seemed quite average, was holding a very dark secret. I was told that her cancer was in and around her sexual organs. I carefully placed my hands on her and almost immediately I began to see images and experience deep emotional feelings. I saw/felt that I was being used in some sort of dark almost Satanic sexual ritual! There was such a vast array of emotions, from excitement, fear, shame and guilt. This all felt as though it was too much for my mind and body to process. I tried using the techniques that I had been practicing, but I could not shed the emotions of the experience.

After the forty five minute session, I felt that I could not share what I had experienced with this woman who had lived it. I went to find Phoenix and ask for her thoughts. I found her alone in her office and she invited me in. As I shared my experience with her, she just sat expressionless looking at me, not giving a clue as to what she might be thinking. When I had finished with my story, I sat waiting for some type of reaction. Was she going to tell me that I was crazy? Was she going to tell me that I had quite an imagination? She looked a little perplexed, but finally acknowledged that what I had seen was what this lady had gone through, and not just one time, but numerous times. Phoenix had been aware of the situation, and I believe she was surprised that I had sensed it so accurately. It was these emotions that this lady was holding inside, that were the very cause of the manifestation of the cancer.

For me, this particular experience was one of the most validating, showing me that I had been truly picking up on other people's experiences. What this lady had gone through, was so far outside of what I would consider to be "normal," that for me to sense it had to mean that I was somehow connecting to other people in a "Mystical" way. Although I did see this lady a couple more times in the compound, I never did share my visions with her. I did not see how in this instance it would have been of benefit for her to know that I was aware of her secret.

Part 3-A Walk-in

It seemed that I had my hands on clients nearly ten hours a day for the weeks that I was there. In many ways, it was amazing to see/feel/sense what these people were holding in their bodies. It gave me such an awareness of how we as humans operate. Every day brought new experiences and deeper understandings. I was so intrigued with this ability that even during breaks and at the end of the workdays, I would offer to "read" the others that were in the class with me, and also the staff that worked at the compound. Although many in my class had been in the healing field for years and each had their own gifts, mine was unique to this group.

It was during these readings that I first became aware of the concept of "Walk-ins." I had not heard this term before, but it seemed that everyone else was quite familiar with it. I was doing a reading on one of my classmates and feeling/sensing a disconnect that was difficult to understand. With my hands on this roughly forty year old man, I was sensing deep traumas from childhood and at the same time sensing him as having very clear energy. It didn't make sense that these past traumas could be in the body and yet somehow not be held in the energy field. During the reading I told myself to look deeper, this was an additional tool that I had learned on my own, that I could ask to go deeper, and I would be taken past the surface level information and into the deepest recesses of the person I would have my hands on. Not long after that, I had visions of this man being with Jesus. I somehow felt/understood that he had been one of the Apostles!

I was told that a "Walk-in" happens when the original soul that was born into a body believes that it cannot stay any longer, usually because the traumas that it has experienced are too great, and they simply don't want to be here. Another soul that had no interest in being born and going through childhood but wants to be here, may step into the body that was no longer wanted. Sometimes both souls may share the body, with the "walk-in" providing strength and comfort to the original occupant. Such was the case with this classmate. He was aware of the life this body had lived and yet even with the physical traumas that had been suffered by the occupied body, he was here to experience a greater human potential. He had been a healer since entering this body and was exploring different modalities of helping himself and others in dealing with afflictions. The body he had chosen was in need of much healing, and he seemed to be in almost constant pain. He was fascinated that I had picked up/seen his life as an Apostle, (a life that he was quite aware of) and he asked questions, testing to see how much of the information I was getting was matching what he recalled from his former lives. As I answered each of his questions, he became more convinced that I was indeed tuning into his former incarnations.

Part 4-To See into the Future

It seemed that the weeks I spent at this amazing place provided one mystical experience after another. Many I witnessed and many were my own to try and make sense of. I had experienced vivid dreams before in my life; dreams that were every bit as real as what we think of as reality. The few times that I had experienced such dreams, they had all come true, most of them the day after having the dream. In the weeks that I was at the class, I had six such dreams. They were as real as if I had actually lived them, and I suspected from my limited experience with this type of dream, that these would also come true. The first of these vivid dreams, I found myself floating through the ceiling and then through the roof of the large room where we worked on the clients. It was evening and the sun had gone down, leaving a beautiful soft light over the buildings and trees in the compound. As I looked around I was surprised to see that most of my classmates were floating there with me. In fact, there were eleven out of the twelve of us hanging out over the building. This was all I remembered about the dream, but it had been so real! How could something this strange actually be lived in reality? Was this going to be my first vivid dream that would not come true?

The very next day, as we finished working with the clients, Phoenix asked us to clear the tables from our work room. We also folded up the massive blue tarp that covered the flooring, leaving the carpet exposed. As we stood around her, she explained that she was going to lead us in a guided meditation. We each grabbed a pillow and stretched out on the floor. I had been meditating for years and was quite familiar with guided ones. Phoenix began by getting us to slow our breathing and relax. After awhile, when she felt we were ready, she instructed us to float up from our bodies, float through the ceiling and up past the roof. There I was, just like in my dream! It was evening and the sun had just disappeared leaving the light exactly as how I had seen it. I looked around to find that there were indeed eleven of us, with one missing.

It was a beautiful meditation that Phoenix guided us through. Although the meditation was very long, the only part that had been in my dream the night before was floating above the room with most of my classmates. Phoenix explained later that the missing classmate was having problems leaving her body, and joining us. So we waited, floating above the roof while Phoenix helped pull her away from her body. This was certainly a wonderful surprise to find that even a dream that would seem to have no way of becoming reality, could actually manifest. Although this one was difficult to see how it could happen, the next vivid dream was even wilder!

Even though every day brought new and exciting experiences, I found that by the end of the day I was exhausted, and ready to climb in bed. I shared my room with two other men, but I found it quite easy to sleep. As I drifted off into the dream world, I felt uneasy. I found myself surrounded by dark beings. They seemed evil and they all had their attention set on me. As I understood that there was no escape, I began to battle these beings. There didn't seem to be a way of defeating them. I would punch one and he would only back up and come at me again, showing no signs that my punch had hurt him at all. I was not sure how many of these evil beings I was fighting, all I knew was that they just kept coming. Then somehow I felt one of them slip inside me! This was one of my vivid dreams and it felt as real as any reality that I have ever experienced. Once this evil energy was inside of me, there was no way of fighting it. I couldn't punch it. I couldn't kick it and I couldn't figure out any way to even threaten it. I could feel the evil thing inside of me laughing with glee over my powerlessness. Then I heard another laugh a little distance away. As I looked toward that laughter, I could see that it was Phoenix. She had been watching the whole battle and was laughing at my situation.

In my late teens, I had gone through some difficult times with very dark energies. I felt them around me almost constantly.

One in particular seemed to sit on my shoulder and would not leave. This lasted for more than a year and it was not only disturbing but often times it had been frightening.

The next day, after having this terrible dream, Phoenix gave us instructions on another type of healing technique. This one involved getting into a specific position with the client and then pulling universal energy through the client, through your own body and then into the Earth. While the rest of my classmates were assigned clients that were dealing with cancer, I was assigned to work on a young lady who looked to be in her mid-twenties. I was not informed of what her difficulties were, only that I was to use this newly learned technique of pulling the universal energy through her and then through me. She got into her position for the work and then I positioned myself as I had been instructed. I found it quite easy to focus on pulling this energy. In fact, I decided to pull it as if the energy were traveling through a fire hose with amazing force.

As I pulled the energy through this young lady and then through me, I began to sense that the universal energy, although pure and beautiful as it entered her, was full of nasty dark energy as it exited her and passed through me. I felt as though she was full of dark energies and that this process was pulling them out of her. Soon, she began to cough and the more energy I pulled through her the harder she coughed. Then I began to cough. It was as though these nasty energies were not happy being evicted and were fighting as they left her body and passed through me. Phoenix was not in the room at the time, but one of her assistants was nearby and came over, concerned over the reactions that my client and I were having. He told me to stop running the energy. I was afraid to stop, because I knew that the stream of energy was filled with dark energy. I knew that if I stopped, that some of that nasty stuff would settle inside me. As long as I was pulling the energy through her and through me, it was leaving me, but if I stopped, where would it go? I felt that stopping the stream would leave some very negative energies trapped inside me.

I followed the instructor's direction, ending the session. As I stood up, I could feel some of that nastiness inside me. For the next few hours, I did not feel like myself. I felt low on energy and moved through those hours as if the very air had thickened to where it took effort to walk through it. My normal level of happiness had diminished to a place where life itself lacked luster. It is difficult to describe the instant change that I felt by stopping that session.

In the evening, Phoenix called all of us back into the main work room. As we all stood waiting to hear what she was going to share, in walked the young lady that I had been working with. She stood next to Phoenix and seemed apprehensive about what might be happening. Phoenix began describing how negative energies, (she called them boogies) could be attracted to a person, and how they can make themselves at home in the right environment. She explained about the things going on in this young woman's life that had allowed many of these boogies to take refuge inside her. Then as we listened and watched, Phoenix performed what I can only describe as an exorcism! The young lady moved violently and made sounds that I had never heard come from a human. After only a minute or two, the woman collapsed to the floor.

If I had not already worked with this lady and experienced the amount of negative energy in her, I would have thought that she and Phoenix were just putting on a show. Yet I was now intimately involved with this "boogie" story. I had felt the energies in her while I was working with her and then felt some of them grab onto me. She was still on the floor when Phoenix began to laugh and turn towards us. I think most of us were still in a minor level of shock after what we had just witnessed, but Phoenix was still laughing and said, "There are still more of these boogies in the room, who is holding them?"

I knew that I was the one holding them, but I had not shared my experience with anyone. How could Phoenix know? She looked directly at me, and I took a step forward, acknowledging that I was indeed the one unwillingly giving refuge to the remainder of the boogies. She walked up to me and it all happened so fast that to this day, I am still not sure exactly what she did. I don't remember if she said anything, but she put her hand to my forehead and the next thing I knew, I was lying on the floor. It felt like I had been hit with an energetic force that washed through me in a millisecond. I instantly felt like myself again. There was space in my body again. There was room for me to be me again.

As I lay in bed that night, I thought about the dream from the night before. I had fought with the evil energies until one had entered me. I remembered that Phoenix had laughed in the dream, just as she had this evening. How could it be possible for dreams to foretell the future? Was this meant to be? Do we have a choice in our future, or is it somehow preordained? These "boogies" were quite nasty ones, but do we all have "boogies" in us, some being nasty and perhaps some even being of benefit? It seemed the more I learned, the less I knew, or at least the more I recognized that I had so much more to learn.

Part 5-A kiss Goodbye

As the days past in this strange and wonderful place, my view of reality was challenged at every turn. Along with the clients that we worked with every day, there were other adventures that Phoenix had planned for us. I experienced my first sweat lodge, my first fire walk and some other events that opened my mind to new possibilities. Every day was something new. One day Phoenix had a gentleman address the class and talk about the use of a divining rod. They are generally used to find underground water, but he was using them in ways that I would not have imagined. He had found that he could locate objects in a city, by laying a map of the city on the floor and using the divining rod over the map. What view of reality would you need to have in order for something like this to be possible?

One night as I slept, I had another of my vivid dreams. This time I was in some type of terminal, like a bus or train terminal. I was with Cristina, a pretty lady that was an assistant in the class. I had chatted with her a couple of times, but not really paid much attention to her since arriving at the compound. In the vivid dream, we were kissing. It was a very passionate kiss, filled with emotion. In the dream, I knew that we had been together for years and loved each other deeply. Our kiss was a kiss good-bye. She was leaving and not wanting to go. I was full of sadness, but knew that she had to leave. The kiss was so vivid that I could actually taste its sweetness.

When I awoke in the morning, the taste of the kiss was still fresh on my lips and in my mind. Up to this point I had hardly noticed her at the compound. We had both been busy, me in the class, and her helping Phoenix behind the scenes. During breakfast, I noticed that she was making a pot of coffee in the break room. She was alone, so I took the opportunity to introduce myself. It is a strange thing to introduce yourself to someone that you know you have loved for years, and yet really know nothing about them. As I stood next to her, I had feelings of not knowing her and memories of years of being lovers. I told her that I had just had a dream about her, and that we had kissed. She smiled and giggled, saying humorously; "Stand in line." This was how we met, from a dream to a beautiful encounter in the break room.

After that, I took every opportunity to spend time with Cristina. We would have lunch together and take walks together. She was so different than any woman I had ever known. She was funny and confident and so independent. Before this class, she had just come back from spending three months in India, most of it on her own. She had travelled to the inner parts of the country on trains, getting a real flavor of the people. She had been born and raised in Mexico City and spoke both English and Spanish perfectly. She had also taken this very class a couple of times and was a wonderful healer.

We did end up getting together, with her moving out to California and living with me for more than eighteen years. I loved her more than words can say. We had many adventures together and shared so many magical times. I had shared with her the dream that had brought us together, and we often joked that as long as we stayed away from terminals, we would be okay. Then one day, she was diagnosed with a terminal illness! There is so much to say about this story, but for now I just want to point out that in my dream we were kissing good-by in a terminal, and it never crossed my mind that the terminal was a terminal disease! Our last kiss was more emotional than I thought a body could handle. My last words to her, "Do you have any idea of how much I love you?" Her last words to me were, "Yes I do, and I am so grateful." Although it took almost nineteen years for this vivid dream to play out, I always knew that our time would end with this kiss.

Part 6-Two Souls

One morning, we were being given our assignments, which consisted of which client we would be working on and how many of us would be working together on each client. I was assigned to a new client, a young woman that I had not worked on before. I was told that she had a small lump on an ovary and that I would be working alone on her. I was directed to a station that had been set up outside. As I approached the outside table, I saw that she was already there waiting for me. We made our introductions and then she reclined onto her back, getting into a comfortable position. I pulled up a chair and sat next to her.

I put my right hand on her, just over the area with the lump. Almost immediately I felt the amazing presence of two joyous spirits that fluttered around this woman like fireflies! They seemed to be so happy to be in her energy field. I had not sensed anything like these two little souls before. They seemed to be pouring out loving support for this woman. I felt so much joy and compassion coming from these two wonderful souls. Their attention was entirely on their host, and they seemed to pay no attention to me. I shared with this woman what I was seeing/sensing. I could see she had tears welling up and at the same time a smile appeared on her face. She understood right away what I was describing to her. She shared with me that she had gone through two abortions.

I could tell that my sharing the joy that these two souls were expressing, gave her some relief. Knowing that they were with her and happy was like a weight lifted from her little body. She explained that although she loved children, her life had been difficult and that she just could not allow herself to bring a child into such an unforgiving world.

It was amazing to experience the presence of these two souls. They only had love for the woman that had not given them the chance to share this physical life with her. There was not an ounce of regret or unhappiness from them. It felt as though these two souls experienced no lack, there was nothing that they needed, only the love and joy that they radiated.

Part 7- My Life's Purpose

As the weeks of training were getting close to finishing, Phoenix asked us to join her in one of the smaller offices. We lined up and then one at a time stood in front of her. As we took turns standing in front of her, she would tell us certain facts about our lives. How she knew such details about us was quite surprising. Then she would tell each person what they had come into this life to experience or accomplish. She literally was telling us what our soul's purpose was! When it was my turn, I walked up and stood before her. She sat looking so regal and so focused. She looked at me and then I could sense her looking into me, almost as though she were looking directly into my soul. Phoenix then shared with me parts of my life that she had somehow tuned into. She explained that through my life, growing up even from being a child that I always wanted to know or understand how things worked. She told me that my passion for understanding such things included life itself, that I was driven to learn the "secrets" of life. She said that it was my soul's purpose to learn, understand and then share with others how and what life was.

To say that I was disappointed at what she had told me would be an understatement. I had taken this class and now had dreams of being a great healer. Although it was true that I had always been someone that wanted to understand how everything worked, where was the excitement in just talking about those things? Being a healer, I could make a difference in people's lives, I could help them solve problems and give them a higher quality of life! I knew that someone could make a good living at being a healer, but how could you make a living talking about life?

I knew that I had been on a quest to have a greater understanding of life since the age of about eighteen. I wanted to know what was of "value" in life. I wanted to know if this life is all that there is, or is there reincarnation or some type of afterlife? I wanted to know what was important in living life, was it being kind, was it learning and acquiring knowledge, was it to make money or become important? I had never considered that my intense desire to find the answers to these questions was for anybody but myself. Now Phoenix was saying that this journey had not been for me alone.

Years later, I was still pondering her words. I was still a general contractor and knew that this work was no longer suited for me. I knew that I had more to offer the world and I needed to find a way to let my contracting business go. It was a fairly successful business where I had such a long list of regular clients that I had not needed to advertise the business in more than seventeen years. This was great in some respects, however it also meant that I had developed relationships with my clients, and that was difficult to let go of.

For decades I had been pursuing my passion for understanding life, but it had slowly become clear that this passion needed to be expressed and shared. As the opportunity would present itself, I found myself giving free readings to anyone willing to let me look into them. With each reading, my understanding of the human experience seemed to grow. I began sharing some of the readings I had done in the past, with people that I somehow knew would benefit from hearing them. Then I started writing many of the readings down until I finally I understood that this story needed to be told. After sharing many of these stories and seeing how they seemed to resonate and touch those that heard them, I finally knew that I needed to put them into a book.

Story #12-Ayahuasca

In 2004, I received an email from a very good friend and spiritual teacher of mine. He was inviting me to attend an event that he was hosting. He had met a Shaman who had introduced him to Ayahuasca. He had somehow convinced this Shaman and his entourage to come to California and lead an Ayahuasca ceremony. I had not heard of Ayahuasca and had no experience with any type of psychedelics.

In high school, most of my friends were into the drug scene, using pot, mushrooms, acid, and other things, but I had no interest. I had no judgments about what they were doing, I just never felt the urge to try any of it. My friends were good friends and never pushed me or judged me for not joining them. I had not ever even tried pot.

Now I have a spiritual teacher that is inviting me to attend a ceremony where the guest of honor is a major psychedelic. I had been on a spiritual search for thirty years that had included daily meditations, reading lots of books, seminars, group meetings and metaphysical events. I had not thought about using drugs to attain any type of spiritual awareness. My friend was quite convincing that this would change my life.

I was given instructions on how to prepare for the event. For several days prior to the ceremony, I was to eat certain types of food and avoid other foods. I was to avoid alcohol and caffeine. I was to drink lots of pure water and show up hydrated. I was to dress in loose, comfortable white clothing. Perhaps the most important thing was I needed to be prepared to surrender.

As I walked into the building where the ceremony was to take place, I saw that there were no chairs, just lots of pillows, cushions and blankets spread around the floor. There was a small table in the center with some small statues of Buddha, some crystals, cups and what had to be the Ayahuasca tea. There were also some musical instruments, including guitars and several types of drums.

When everyone had arrived, we each found a comfortable spot on the floor with our cushions and blankets. We were also each given a small white bucket. My friend stood up and introduced the Shaman. He was a very pleasant looking man in his mid-thirties. He had such a look of peace and confidence about him. He introduced his entourage, several very lovely young women and a young man. They had each already grabbed one of the musical instruments, and it became obvious that we were to have live music. The Shaman gave us a little history of Ayahuasca, which he always referred to as "the medicine." He explained how every plant has something to teach us, but that Ayahuasca was considered the "Mother of all teacher plants." He explained how for instance Peyote connects us with mother earth and animals, but that Ayahuasca connects us with our God Self.

My friend had told me that no matter what happened during the ceremony, if I wanted the best experience, I needed to surrender. I thought I knew what surrender was, but over the next four to five hours, I was to find out that I had no idea about the levels of surrender that were possible! That surrender meant letting go of everything that I thought was me, letting go of everything that I had a "Point of View" about. Letting go of what I thought was real.

The ceremony began with the entourage playing the most beautiful music and singing and sometimes chanting. While they were playing, we each got up and walked to the table for our first taste of the tea. The Shaman would look at each of us and decide how full to fill our cup, some getting a quarter cup and others as much as a full cup. We would drink the tea, hand the cup back to the Shaman and return to our seat.

I sat with my legs crossed and tried to be as spiritual looking as I could be. I was enjoying the live music which just went from one amazing song to another. I had been sitting there for probably fifteen minutes and thinking that there was nothing to this Ayahuasca stuff. I had not noticed a thing. Then I started to feel an unusual sensation in my stomach. It was like a warm burning feeling. Then I felt somewhat lightheaded. For some reason, I looked at my right hand and was amazed by what I was seeing. It was as though I was seeing my hand clearly for the first time in my life. In a way it was as if I were looking through a microscope, where I could see every hair and the hole that the hair was growing out of. I could have spent hours just investigating my hand! But the medicine had much more in store for me.

As I closed my eyes, the most amazing geometric patterns had formed. It was almost like in the movie the "Matrix" (which had not come out yet) Neo was seeing the patterns that make up the world that we know. Walls, floors, people, everything was made of these beautiful bright shining geometric patterns. I opened my eyes and felt so out of control that for a moment I began to panic. Then I remembered my friend telling me that no matter what happened, no matter what I saw, SURRENDER.

Suddenly it felt as though I fell backward, I knew that I was still sitting, but the larger part of me was falling backward into empty space. I surrendered to the falling and actually enjoyed the unbelievable feeling of tumbling through space backward.

For about the next hour (time had no meaning at that point) I found myself saying "Oh My God" as some new revelation was shown me, or I would just let out a "WOW," as I grasped some new way of understanding life. Life was making sense in ways that I had never imagined. There seemed to be part of me that understood each of the revelations and that part of me would think, "How could I have forgotten this." It was as though these "secrets" of life were perfectly obvious, but they had somehow been wiped from my memory. Now as they were being shown to me, I found myself amazed that I could have ever forgotten them.

Over and over I found that what I was surrendering was ego. By ego, I mean the "rightness" that I had about almost everything. We spend our lives deciding what is right and what's wrong. This person treated me poorly, so I am right to be hurt or angry. I am a man and certain behaviors are how men are supposed to act and other behaviors are less than manly. Many of my beliefs about "rightness" came from personal experience, but many came from my parents, my friends or my teachers. Now the medicine was telling me to let go of these made up points of view. It was my ego that held these points of view, and as I would surrender one, I would feel such an expanse in my beingness. It was almost as though each point of view was holding my true being in contraction. Then as it was released, that contraction would let go and I would experience a sense of expansion. At times, I would revel in my accomplishment of letting go of ego, only to recognize that it was my ego that was reveling. I thought I knew what surrender was, but I really had no idea of the depth that surrender could go, or that one point of view may have to be surrendered over and over.

At the end of the first hour, we were invited back up to the table for a second round of the medicine. I was so deep into the experience, I am not sure how I was able to stand up and get myself to the table and back to my seat. I was concerned at what this second round of the medicine would do to me considering how profound of an effect the first dose had on me. I sat with my legs crossed and tried to prepare myself for whatever was to come. Soon I felt the familiar sensation in my stomach and was off on another adventure.

There are no words in the English language that could adequately describe what happened next. I was experiencing what I can only describe as total Oneness! I was one with God, the Universe, All That Is, I was Infinite! There is no separation in infiniteness. There are no objects to perceive, no sounds to hear, no fragrances to smell, there is only beingness. There was no sense of an individual self, no memory of the me that I had been. There was only infinite peace. I call it peace, but joy, love or happiness all work to describe true beingness. Time no longer existed, nor did space, these were concepts that did not apply to the Infinite.

Suddenly, there was a sense of self again. There was an "I," an individual somehow separate from the Infinite and yet a knowing that it was impossible to be separate from All That Is. I understood that the "I" that was being experienced was still within God, but I had an individual point of view. That meant that there could be the experience of separation. There could be objects to perceive and sensations to be felt. It was almost painful to feel this separate from God, and yet to have a point of view as a separate self was intoxicating. With a point of view, time could now exist, and so could space. I understood that from a point of view, cause and effect now applied. I could "do" something and it would have an effect on another thing.

I did not have a form, nor was I perceiving any objects. I did seem to have an awareness that at the same time that I was given this sense of individuality, that there were eleven more individual awarenesses that came into being. I somehow knew that these others were different from the "I" that I was being. I could see/sense that they were going to be exploring realities, dimensions, ways of being vastly different from what was in store for me. Even though I had no concept of planets, people or matter, there was a knowing, that I would/could experience many lifetimes and adventures but that at some point I would gladly, lovingly give it up to go back into the totality of the Infinite.

Periodically, I would open my eyes and be back in the room and see the others, each having their own experience with the medicine. At these times, with my eyes open, I would feel such connection with everyone. Perhaps the only word that truly describes the connection that I was feeling, is LOVE. I had no point of view about these people. Whatever was going on in their life story was of little consequence. All that seemed important was that we had all chosen to be here together. Here in this room, here in this lifetime, here in this seemingly physical reality, on a seemingly real planet. There was an understanding, that just being here, in a reality that seemed to keep us separate from each other and from the wholeness of God, caused a certain level of suffering.

As part of my journey with the medicine, I became aware of so much suffering. Simply to experience life as a separate individual being, was cause enough to suffer. On top of that, we behave in ways that cause so much suffering for others and for ourselves. The more that I understood this suffering, the more I felt my heart open for humanity, for myself and all living creatures. There was a recognition that we had all chosen to be here, in spite of the pain, we were here to experience the contrast together. As I looked around the room, I loved each person, felt their pain and had such compassion for the amount of courage it took them to be here.

The medicine brings up deep emotions, toxins, fears that have been trapped in the body. It is quite common to "purge" as part of the cleansing process. Often as a particular emotion is brought up, you can feel the purge begin. In one instance, I saw myself as a very dark skinned angry, cruel man. I was standing over a woman who was cowering before me on the ground. I had a whip in my hand and I was using it on her. I had such rage, not that this woman had wronged me in any way, it was just a rage about life. As I struck her again with the whip, I felt such shame well up inside me. How could I ever make amends for such an act? I felt the shame build and it became the impetus for a purge. The medicine had shown me the darkness that I had held from some other lifetime, and now it was giving me the opportunity to purge it from my body. I purged and wept at the same time.

Each time I opened my eyes and looked around the room, the women seemed to catch more of my attention. When I would hold my gaze on any of the women, I would begin to feel their pain. No doubt we were all here working with the medicine in hopes of healing some of our own suffering. It became apparent to me, that in so many ways, this earthly life is harder on women, and the level of suffering seems to be greater for them.

The medicine showed me the amazing gifts that women bring to this reality. It showed me that they are willing to suffer greater to bring love, beauty and compassion into this contrasting world. They are the glue that binds families, communities and countries. As I would look at each of the women in the ceremony, I would feel their struggle and their strength. It was such an honor to experience their light in this way. Over the last sixteen years, I have worked with the medicine eight times. Each and every time, the medicine made sure that I experienced the beauty and grace of women. I could no longer see any woman without remembering who they are. The saddest part of this experience is that so few women understand this about themselves. So few love and appreciate their womanhood.

Through the entire ceremony, the music had continued and had lifted me to so many beautiful awarenesses and understandings. It had been as if the music created wings for my soul to fly to heights that I had no idea existed. The energy of the Shaman and the amazing entourage that accompanied him, filled the room with lightness and joy. Their singing had been so inspiring and uplifting. As the music and ceremony was ending, people began standing and mingling. I, however, was still as deep into the medicine as I had been at any point. As I watched them moving around and visiting with each other, I was still in a place of total oneness and love for each of them. It was as if the veil of separateness had been lifted and I could see and experience everyone in the greater context of who we really are.

I stretched my body down on the floor and pulled a blanket over me, not wanting to let this wonderful experience slip away in conversation. I closed my eyes and allowed myself to be bathed in the Oneness as I drifted off to sleep.

For anyone considering working with the medicine, I would suggest finding a Shaman that has been working with it and understands the power and benefits of Ayahuasca. I have worked with the medicine in eight ceremonies, and I would only do such work in ceremony and with a Shaman.

My dear friend had been so right! This experience had indeed changed my life in so many ways and I am eternally grateful for his invitation to know life in a much greater and profound way. Each time it was amazing to see how we would arrive for a ceremony as individual people filled with points of views and walls of protection, only to have the medicine cleanse these things from our souls and expose the truth of just how connected we really are.

Story #13-A Class in Consciousness

In 2016, I took a class called "Transcending the Levels of Consciousness." The instructor was a wonderful woman with a real gift for teaching and such an abundance of calm patience. The class followed the teachings of Dr. David Hawkins. The premise of the teaching was that as individual people inhabiting Planet Earth, we are not all on the same "Level of consciousness." Dr. Hawkins has come up with a scale and assigned the levels from 0 to 1,000. No person on the planet would be at a level 0, and even the low level of 100 would be very unusual. Jesus and Buddha would be examples of the levels nearing 1000.

According to Dr. Hawkins, the average level of consciousness for the entire population of the planet is around 200. Below this level, people are in more of a survival mode and live in a world of fear, shame, guilt and unworthiness. Above the 200 level, people are turning their attention to questions of Spirit, asking, "Why am I here?" "What am I to do with my life"? The higher the level of consciousness, the more the heart is open and the more we see the Devine in all things.

When someone is living in the lower levels of fear, shame, guilt or unworthiness, it is quite difficult to move into or even be aware that higher levels are possible. They may not even have the life energy to move into a higher level. Most of the time, help is needed for them to overcome the emotional weight that they are carrying. During the class, the instructor would describe different scenarios and situations that we have all experienced in life and then relate that to a particular level of consciousness. Then she would ask, "What would it take to move to the next higher level?" For instance, if you have been in a love relationship and that relationship has ended, you might be experiencing fear of being alone, unworthiness, possibly guilt or other lower level emotions. From this dark, heavy place, what would it take to move out of such emotions and into a happier experience? For many of us, we might believe that we can't be happy until we find another "Love" to fill the void. We believe that since we lost the object of our happiness, we must find another object to replace the missing bringer of joy.

As the instructor would describe such scenarios and then ask, "What would it take to move into a higher level," I would give my answer, "It would take an act of God!" In the beginning, this answer was somewhat sarcastic, but soon I realized that it was indeed always the right answer. An act of God is the opening of the heart, and that opening always leads to a higher level of experience.

All too often, instead of opening the heart, we tend to build more walls to protect ourselves from further hurt. This direction always keeps us in the lower levels of emotion and blocks us from moving into a higher level of consciousness. This single revelation has helped me every time that I have felt stuck in the denseness of emotions. As much as my mind wants to go round and round, justifying my "Rightness," that I should feel fear, anger, betrayed or unworthy, those very thoughts are what keep us locked in the lower levels of experience. It is only by surrendering these heavy emotions that we can move beyond them. It is that act of surrender that is the opening of the heart. It is the act of surrender that allows the flow of happiness to move into our experience. It is always the act of surrender that moves us to a higher level of consciousness, where life becomes fuller, more open and more peaceful.

Surrender is often looked at as weakness. We envision a battle where the one that surrenders is the loser and the one that does not give up is the victor. Yet surrender is the greatest tool we have to attain happiness, peace and fulfillment. What we surrender in order to reach higher vibrations of being, are all the things that are limiting beliefs about who and what we truly are.

If we were to look at our level of consciousness as a vibration, and the higher the level of consciousness the higher frequency of vibration, and then picture a time when you felt real joy, perhaps as a child being tickled, you would be vibrating at roughly the level of 540. According to Dr. Hawkins scale of consciousness, joy is at the 540 level, a rather high vibration. At the level of joy life would feel expansive, light and wonderful. Now remember a time when you behaved in a way that caused your parents to be angry, perhaps to the point of getting a spanking and being told that you should be ashamed of yourself. Shame is at the very low level of just 20 and guilt is just above that at 30. At these low levels there is barely enough life energy or frequency to survive and if we were to stay at such a low level it would feel like life is not worth living. At a very early age, most of us experienced these drastic vibrational highs and lows. The memories of each of these vibrations are stored and easily accessed when we turn our attention to those memories.

For most of us, life becomes a series of highs and lows. Now thanks to Dr. Hawkins' work, it becomes evident that a "low" is not just a feeling, but an actual decrease of vibration and life energy. A "high" is an increase to a higher vibration and therefore greater flow of life energy. What we want to surrender are these low vibration thoughts and emotions, yet while we are in the midst of experiencing shame, our minds are telling us over and over all the reasons that we should feel shame. How can you surrender something that you believe you deserve? While shame is an emotion, it is kept alive by all the thoughts that tell us we are unworthy of anything else, and because shame lowers our vibration and energy flow, we most likely do not feel that we have enough life energy to help ourselves move out of this very low level. It is generally with the help of family, friends or professionals that we are able to move out of such situations. Perhaps those helping us move forward are the "act of God" that seemed to always be the right answer. They help us open our hearts and recognize a higher vibration.

Even to move from the very high level of Joy at 540, to the level of Peace at 600 takes an act of God. While Joy is wonderful, the level of Peace takes us to a vibration of higher understanding. This is a level where Peace is experienced even in the midst of chaos. We are more connected with God and have a greater awareness of the perfection in all things. So, to move from Joy to Peace, surrender is necessary, and in fact surrender is the only tool that we have to open our hearts and allow higher vibrations to move us.

One day after celebrating a birthday, I had several helium balloons left over from the party. I took one of the balloons and tied a weight to it, leaving a tail of ribbon below the weight. I was able to get the balloon balanced to the point where it was floating right about eye level. For several days this balloon would float around the house freely. It was kind of fun not knowing when and where I might run into it. It was almost like it had become alive and a joyous friend. I would be deep in thought and turn a corner in the house only to run right into the balloon. My mind would shift from my very serious thoughts, to enjoying the freedom of the balloon travelling through my home and being moved by the most gentle of air flows. As the helium slowly drained from my friend, I would cut another section of ribbon tail until it was floating back freely at eye level again.

Using Dr. Hawkins scale of consciousness and seeing how we can equate the level of consciousness with a level or frequency or vibration, we might notice that as we are born into this world we are as free as the balloon. We are at a high level of vibration as we begin to learn or understand that we now "inhabit" a physical body. We have come from a place of openness and oneness into a world of contrast. There is now me and then everything else. We now have experiences of separateness, need and lack. Feeling separate becomes a weight on our balloon. Feeling lack becomes another weight, and as we begin to experience more of this physical world, more weights are added until we are no longer floating, but being dragged across the floor.

When we add the weights of shame or guilt or grief we might become stuck in one place, and even a good breeze may not be enough to drag us any farther. Using this example, it is easy to see that until we surrender some of the weight, we are not going anywhere. These weights are not going to magically disappear, they can only be released. Release happens through surrender, we are literally deciding to surrender things that are of no service to us. Why would we ever choose to hang on to weights that keep us from the freedom of floating?

It is as we reach the levels above 200 that our balloon begins to float. We begin to see life from a higher perspective. We see that life does not have to be a constant struggle. As we look around from this higher vantage point we feel lighter and happier. As our balloon begins to float we can feel the movement or flow of life. The level of 200 is denoted by the feeling of "Courage." From this level life is less frightening and we feel empowered to venture into new endeavors. Still, this is just the level of 200 and there are so many more levels to open up to. Dr. Hawkins' scale has Love at 500, Joy at 540,

Peace at 600, and Enlightenment at 700. It may take lifetimes to move from 200 to the level of 300. Yet I believe that we all experience glimpses of the higher levels, like when we feel unconditional love for a child, or when we are laughing with total joy. At the moment that we are laughing with joy, we are not focused on the problems of life, we are caught up in the present moment of just joy. We have temporarily surrendered some of our weights and experience a much higher vibration. Then as we once again focus on the weights of life we are brought right back to where we started.

I live in the mountains in California, and most days I walk about a mile and half to my mailbox and back. It is a dirt/gravel road in what would be considered a forest area. I pass several houses on this walk, each cared for in a different way. Some yards are kept so neat, and others left more like the natural forest, with trees that have died and fallen over, surrounded by tall weeds and grass. In parts of the road the trees form what seems like a tunnel, and in other areas there are openings through the trees where I can see the sky and surrounding mountains. I have been practicing walking sections of the road keeping my mind clear from thoughts. This means walking without thinking, walking without words in my head. At first it was difficult to look ahead and see the road, the houses, the trees, the sky, and the animals without giving each a name or category. To not think the word tree or sky or blue or beautiful was at first a challenge. It was also a challenge to not think about what I needed to do that day, or of events happening around the world. At first I would tell myself that from this tree to the driveway up ahead I would keep my mind clear. Then as I got better at this practice, I could go longer distances and it began to feel natural to walk without words.

I found that walking in silence somehow made awareness expand. When I was looking at a tree without labeling it a tree, the separation between what I thought myself to be, and what I thought a tree to be, disappeared. I could look at the sky and the trees and road, and there was now only the experience of the moment. Everything was simply happening in the totality of the present now. I experienced a deep sense of peace and wholeness. I am not sure of the vibration level or consciousness level that I was experiencing, I only know that it was profoundly peaceful. I tell this story so that we might look at this experience to explore the levels of consciousness.

If we were to be taking this same walk to the mailbox and be thinking about how man has helped to facilitate climate change, we might see how so many trees are struggling, and many have fallen from the drought, the heat, and the constant attack from insects. We might begin to feel guilt for what humans are doing to the planet. We might feel shame for being part of the problem, for driving a gas burning vehicle or not doing more to stop the destruction of the forests. It is possible to think these thoughts and begin to feel the emotions of guilt or shame, and lower our life vibration to shame at 20, or guilt at 30. At the end of the walk we would arrive back home feeling depleted and unhappy.

If we were to be taking this same walk to the mailbox and be thinking about how dry the trees and grasses are, we might be thinking about how every year seems to bring more and larger fires to California. We might begin to feel fear about the possibility of a fire that could destroy much of the forest and the cozy homes. We might feel anger that our government isn't doing more to prevent such disasters. Fear is a vibration of 100 and anger is 150. These vibrations are much higher than that of shame or guilt, yet they are still very low on the vibrational scale. At the end of the walk we might arrive back home quite upset and unhappy.

If we were to take this same walk feeling proud, thinking about how as humans we have been able to carve areas out the forest, and build amazing homes with running water, heat and electricity. We might still notice the dead trees and be aware of how we are also contributing to climate change. At the level of pride, a vibration of 175, or courage at 200, we might see all this as just another challenge that mankind will overcome. We have the energy and the courage to look to a brighter future. As we return home, we might feel uplifted from our walk and hopeful for what is to come.

If we were to take this walk and be thinking about accepting that we as humans are always evolving, and learning, and that we are still trying to find ways of living in harmony with nature. We might feel appreciation for the dance of life, the flow of life and death, and see it all as the movement of consciousness. We might believe that mankind will be able to "reason" its way to solutions for the damage that it has brought to this planet. That by using the power of reason we can accomplish what might have seemed impossible. Acceptance is a vibration of 350 and reason is at the level of 400. As we arrive back home, we might feel energetic from the movement of walking, and an inner calmness, and appreciation for the dance of life.

If we were to take this same walk and be thinking and feeling love for all the life around us, including appreciation for the struggles we all face in undertaking this journey, we might be radiating a vibration of love that joins us with all that we see. We might even begin to be filled with the joy that we are able to experience the wonderful world around us. As we walk, we might be aware of how the climate is changing. We understand that nothing ever stays the same. We know that mankind is linked to the planet, and all of its inhabitants. We can see how with greater awareness of how everything is connected, mankind will find a way of living in harmony with nature. Love is a vibration of 500 and Joy is at 540. As we arrive back home, we might be feeling completely fulfilled and joyful about life. We might feel that we are in harmony with whatever life brings us.

As we look at how our experience of the walk is so dramatically different depending on what, and how, we are thinking and feeling, we might begin to understand the importance of our thoughts. In each case, we could see that our thoughts reflect a level of truth. During the first walk where we are focused on the damage that mankind has caused, and we are feeling guilt or shame, we might notice that we have placed our attention on a very specific "part" of the truth. As we are focused on this limited truth, our vibration is lowered to reflect the feelings of guilt or shame. At this level we are unable to grasp that there might be a "greater" truth. We are stuck in this low vibration, and all of life around us reflects that vibration back to us.

During the second walk when we were feeling fear or anger, we were placing our attention on circumstances that in our beliefs could be different. We could see that at some point mankind could move to address the damages that we are causing. The vibrations of fear and anger are much higher than guilt or shame. From this higher vibration of anger there is a flicker of hope for a better future. Instead of being stuck in the "truth" as seen from the vibration of guilt, we now see a larger truth that includes hope.

During the third walk, where we are experiencing pride or courage, we are still aware of the damage that mankind has caused, however from here we see a greater truth. We see that mankind has made many amazing accomplishments, and that when we have been faced with challenges, we somehow find a way to overcome them. From this vibration of courage, our view of the "truth" is much greater. There is not just hope, but the evidence of the past has shown that we can and will prevail. The "truth" at this level is expanded and far less limited than the "truth" viewed through the level of shame.

During the fourth walk where we were experiencing acceptance or reason, we are aware of the same circumstances as with all of the other walks, but we were no longer in resistance to "what is." At this level there is an acceptance, that whatever is happening now, is the starting point for where and how we move forward. We are not locked into seeing the past as an indication of where we are going. We simply acknowledge where we are and look to ways of creating life better. From this vibration of reason, our view of the "truth" is so expanded that it hardly feels as though there are limits on it.

During the fifth walk while we are experiencing love and joy, it is as though we have stepped back and can see life in a greater totality. "Truth" is experienced as the movement of life. There is an ebb and flow, and at each end love is not lost. Love is experienced as the truth of life. The same understandings of climate change and human influence on the environment are hardly viewed as obstacles. There is more like an acknowledgement of where we are in the "flow." In the vibration of love at 500, and joy at 540, we return home with the same energy as we started with. Not only are we vibrating at this amazing level, but we shared this vibration with the world as we took our walk.

We have been taught that there is only one truth, but for most of us, there was never a mention, that the one truth could be viewed from different perspectives. In fact everything that we experience is always viewed from a particular point, from our own "point of view." To understand that how we look at something literally makes all the difference in how our lives unfold, is to give us a tool for improving our lives. The one clear way of knowing what level of consciousness we are experiencing at any moment, is to look at how we are feeling! If we are feeling guilt, our life energy is low and life itself is viewed as hopeless. At this level our minds will go round and round reminding us of all the reasons that we should feel guilty and unworthy. If we are feeling proud, our life energy is higher and life is viewed as being filled with possibilities. If we are feeling love, the world itself is amazing. At this level life energy is flowing into us and pouring out into the world.

Just remembering that our feelings and emotions are telling us how we are perceiving, and interacting with the world, we might begin to view our emotions as messages, indicating how narrow, or how expanded our "truth" is. Another simple way of looking at it, is to imagine putting on a pair of glasses that block out everything except for an opening the size of a BB. What you see through this small hole is true, but very limited. The larger the hole placed in the glasses, the greater amount of truth is viewed. In each case, we believe that we are seeing the entire truth, yet even at the level of Love at 500, we are still only able to view the world, or reality from the limits of the vibration of Love. It is most likely not possible to see the entire truth of anything, as long as we are in human form.

Dr. Hawkins' book, "Transcending the Levels of Consciousness" gives us a truly wonderful way of understanding each other and a new way of seeing ourselves.

Truth can only ever be seen from the point that it is being viewed and can never be the entire truth. This means that whatever your perception of the truth is, it will always be limited. Just having this one understanding makes it easier to surrender our limited view, knowing that it is always limited, and reach for a higher understanding, a higher place to view our truth from.

Story #14-The Eternal Now

It was a normal summer morning. I had gotten up from bed, fed the kitties, made coffee, and sat on the couch with my lovely Cristina. We sipped our coffees while I slipped into a meditation and began describing what my guide was showing me. I don't believe that I have ever had two meditations where similar things were shown to me. It is hard to imagine that there could be so many messages and so many ideas, that every day could be a brand new one.

There have been precious few times that, as I would connect with my guide, I would feel my head being pulled back so that my face was looking up towards the ceiling. Each time this had happened, I felt my energy being drawn upwards, and meeting what I have always felt was a higher guide, a guide to my guide perhaps. I could feel that this guide or energy was working to lower its vibration to a level that I could connect with. The reality that this guide occupied was so foreign to the physical life that I knew, and I could only feel moments of such expanse and openness to provide hints as to what that reality must be like. It seemed as if this connection was being made possible by my "normal" guide. It felt as though he was acting as a platform for this higher guide and I to meet.

The things that I would experience while connected to this higher vibrational being, had more to do with the expanse of awareness, and very little to do with physical life. While my normal guide would show me ways of connecting with planet Earth and all of its many inhabitants, this higher guide seemed to have little interest in the earthly limitations. In this higher realm, there did not even seem to be objects. It was more about energy and exploring awareness itself. An interesting point in connecting with this guide was that since his realm seemed to have no objects, there also was no language. There was no need for a word because words are used to describe things, and there were no things to describe. Instead, there were ways of being and feeling. For instance, while connected with this guide I might feel awareness focus to such a finite point and then expand beyond the limits of an entire universe. I could feel connections with other beings that seemed to occupy this vibration. It felt as if there was such a love for each of these beings and yet there seemed to be no separation between them and me.

I have to admit that there simply are no words that could ever describe the reality that this higher being occupied. Even to use the words "higher being" is so inaccurate, as is the word occupied, but I only have words to make a feeble attempt at some form of description. Just as I have described my guide as being my higher self, it also feels as though this higher guide is still a higher vibration of me, or more accurately I am a lower vibration of that higher self. There seems to somehow be this recognition that we are in fact one and the same.

The "messages" that I have received from these higher meditations revolve around the awareness of how limited our finite world of matter is. Our attention is split into what we see, feel, hear, taste, smell, think, remember and worry about. There is very little of our time that is spent being present and focused. It is almost as if every little thing in our world is asking to be noticed, whether it is a cat, a tree, a lake, a sound, a thought, a memory or a desire. We flitter from one thing to another, not understanding how precious our attention is.

Each time I have connected with this higher guide I have felt so expansive and open. It seems to take a little bit of time for me to fall back into the trap of splitting my attention again. For awhile I am floating in such peace and space, and my mind is not looking for anything to attach to. So as this meditation ended, I was once again feeling the expanse and peace. My mind was quiet and at rest. Cristina and I finished our coffees and began getting ready for the day. It was a Saturday, and I did not have to go to work. I helped make breakfast, and we had a lovely meal, sitting at the table and sharing our thoughts.

After doing the dishes I headed into the bedroom to get dressed. There are double doors at the entry to the bedroom and since we live alone the doors are almost always left open. Just as I stepped through the doorway into the bedroom my world vanished! Again, it is so difficult to put into words what I experienced, but I was no longer in the bedroom, nor was I in the house or even in the world that I had been in just a moment before. I stopped moving, having no perception of the room that I knew I was standing in. Instead of seeing the room, I was suddenly in what I understood to be the eternal now! Time and space no longer existed. I understood that everything that has ever happened or will ever happen was all here. Not just the events of Earth, but everything, everywhere was present. It was a vast expanse of total awareness. It seemed life and energy were moving all around me. Infinite lives and events were present and taking place. Perhaps the closest description would be to walk into a large theater where every movie ever made was being played at the same time. Billions of voices all speaking clearly and yet unless I focused on one, I would not understand what was being said.

This all happened so fast and lasted only seconds. It felt as though I recognized that what I was perceiving, was all quite common and natural. I also felt as though my physical mind could not hold on to this experience for more than a few seconds. It felt as though my mind was both absolutely full and empty at the same time. There was this infinite expanse and yet so much activity. I even felt like I could perceive an infinite number of voices, of lives, of experiences all happening in a single moment.

After a few seconds the experience began to fade until I was back in my bedroom again. For the next few minutes, I stood there processing what had just happened. Part of me could still hear the voices and I made a half-hearted attempt to return to the experience. I quickly realized that this was a gift from my higher guide and had been made possible through the earlier meditation. As I took a step forward towards my bathroom, I felt almost as though I were drunk. My legs were not quite steady, and it took several more minutes before I felt reconnected with my body.

This experience took place a few years ago, and yet it is as real today as it was back then. I often ponder how life can exist without time and space. There have been moments when it seemed all quite clear, and then times when I would find myself trying to understand again. It seems that for now, I have to accept that my finite mind is not capable of conceiving of, or retaining the idea of the infinite.

Story #15-The Meditation that challenged me on multiple levels

In the summer of 2001, I had awakened early one morning and quietly climbed out of bed, leaving my girlfriend sleeping, and headed to the living room. I was feeling refreshed after a great night's sleep and thought it would be a perfect time to meditate. I positioned myself on the couch, sitting with my legs crossed, and began to let go of all thoughts. With the house quiet, it was easy to slip into the expanse of the void. I felt my guide was with me, so I decided to let him take me on an adventure. I had done this many times, and he would take me deep into the recesses of my body, or off into the infinite void, and show me such amazing scenes, or lead me to some mind-blowing awareness.

This time was completely different! Instead of going within or up, he was leading me down into the depths of the Earth. Instead of feeling free and light, the deeper we went the heavier and more contracted I felt. I felt uneasy, and yet I knew as long as my guide was with me, I was safe. We continued diving into the solidity of the earth, going deeper and deeper. Finally, we arrived in some caverns that seemed to be honeycombed, and went on for vast distances.

In all of my meditations involving my guide, we had always gone into the most marvelous and expansive places. He had never taken me to a place where I felt unsafe. Every previous meditation had brought me to an experience of opening my heart and understanding things in new and more expansive ways. This time things were very different. As I turned to ask why he had brought me here, to a place that felt like the depths of Hell, I was shocked to see/feel that he was no longer with me! I did a quick scan of all that surrounded me, and sure enough my guide was nowhere to be found! I was alone in these dark caverns, or so I thought. I could feel myself being consumed by fear. It crept up my body like I had just been immersed in ice water. Thoughts flew through my head as I tried to understand what was going on. Why had I been brought here, and why did my guide leave me?

I'm not sure if I heard a noise or if I had somehow detected movement behind me, but I turned around to find two hideous creatures approaching me. They were moving from the black emptiness of the tunnel behind, and staring right at me! These creatures looked very much like the creature Gollum from Lord of Rings, but Gollum had somewhat of a cuteness about him, while these two creatures looked empty, as though all of the life force had been drained from them. I looked quickly in each direction, hoping to find an avenue of escape, but there was just this one tunnel. A thought entered my mind, "This must be a test!" My guide would not have left me here to die; he must have believed that I was capable of handling whatever was about to happen. As I faced the two creatures, I could feel their pain, their fears, their loneliness and even their longing for a better life. They tried to act aggressive and make me fear them, but it was too late, I had already felt how afraid they were. I knew that they had no power to harm me. I could feel my own energy level and understood that the power that I possessed was far greater than anything that they had available. As they realized that I was not going to be afraid of them, one turned and slowly walked back into the darkness of the tunnel. The other stepped towards me and pleaded with me to take him out of this horrible place.

As I looked around, there was only solid rock, and this tunnel that meandered through it. I knew that I was still deep in meditation, and that reality was only how I perceived it. I thought about my options, and suddenly had the idea that I could jump up through the ceiling of the tunnel, and SWIM through the rock of the Earth. I looked at the poor creature in front of me and wondered how long he had been trapped here; a lifetime, two lifetimes, or perhaps even longer. I told him of my plan to fly through the ceiling of the tunnel, and swim to the surface, but even as I explained what I was going to attempt to do, I recognized that this was a test for me. Would I have the energy, the WILL to swim through miles of earth and rock? As I looked at this soul in front of me, I knew that he would not have the strength or the will to make such a journey. I could see that he also recognized that it would be beyond his power to accompany me without my help. I could sense his sadness and despair at being left there for another lifetime, or even longer.

I wondered if this was part of my "Test." Was I being tested to see if I had enough compassion to help this creature? Was I willing to risk my own life, for the life of another? I thought about taking his hand and pulling him along with me, but I knew that he did not have enough strength even to be pulled. As I was pondering over what to do, he pointed to my chest, with eyes that pleaded for me to help him. I looked down at my chest and could see that it was illuminated, light was radiating out from my heart center. I knew that this was the center of my power, and that this creature was asking me to reach in, and take some of it out, and hand it to him. I wondered about sharing my personal power, and if I did, could we both have enough strength, and will, to reach the surface? Part of me knew that this would be very risky, and that by taking this creature with me, we were risking both of our lives.

For me the choice was a simple one, I could not be the person that I believed myself to be and leave this poor creature here. If I were to leave him in this dark place, I would forever look back, and regret my decision. Whatever was going to happen, we were going to leave this place together. I reached into my heart and pulled half of my power out. I handed the glowing treasure to my companion and as he touched it I could see life energy flow from it into him. His eyes began to light up and even a type of smile seemed to form on his withered face. I took his hand and launched us both up through the ceiling of the cave.

At first it felt awkward trying to swim through rock. I tried different types of strokes that I had known from swimming in water, but this was different, I was not swimming at the surface of water and trying to keep my head above it. I was deep, deep underground. The weight of the earth and rock could easily crush my flesh and bone body. I was swimming upward and none of the normal strokes seemed to work very well. As I struggled to adapt to the reality of swimming in rock, my companion suddenly let go of my hand! I looked down and could see him descending back towards the tunnel. I understood in that moment, he had made the decision that our journey was too frightening for him. I could sense his glee at going back to his life in the tunnel with half of my power, half of my life force. With such power, he would be like a king among the drained souls.

I looked upward again and resumed my search for the proper stroke. Soon my body began to fall into a very natural rhythm of swimming like a dolphin. Yes, this was the right method. It felt so natural, and so powerful. Somehow my body seemed to remember swimming this way, almost as though I had been a dolphin before. I moved through the earth with ease, and at times it almost felt as though my body was buoyant and being pulled upward.

After swimming this way for awhile, I began to get tired. I thought about how I had given half of my power, half of my life force, to the creature who was now so far below me, most likely back in the tunnels where we had met. I knew that I still had miles to go to reach the surface, but my energy was fading fast. How I longed to have my full energy back. I slowed my pace in hopes of conserving some energy. The slower my pace, the more I felt the density of the earth. Instead of sliding through the rocks, there were times and places that it felt like a rock would reach out and try to grab me. I was beginning to feel the friction of the ground and it slowed my pace even more. Finally I came to a complete stop! The very instant that my movement upward ceased, I felt the rocks close in on me. I knew that if I wasn't able to resume my swim soon, I would be trapped in the solidity of the earth, with little hope of ever escaping. At least the creatures below had tunnels to move around in, but if I were to get stuck here, even moving a hand would become impossible.

I took a long deep breath and forced my body onward. Just the short break seemed to have given me more energy. I thought about how this was a test and that my guide must have known that I would be able to get back home. I envisioned being surrounded by light and was once again swimming upward at a rapid pace, feeling light and free. I sensed that I had passed the halfway point, and just thinking about how I now had less than half of the weight of the rocks on top me, helped me to feel like I could go all the way. Then once again I could feel my energy fading, and my pace began to slow. This time I felt that if I came to a complete stop, I would not be able to get started again! I cleared the fear from my mind and tried to fill my body with every ounce of energy that I could find. I was again moving upward, but my life force felt so weak, and depleted.

It's a strange feeling to have completely exhausted your life energy. It felt as though the essence that was me, was being scattered into the earth around me. I had no choice, my body came to a stop and the earth grabbed me from every direction. With so little energy, it seemed that my body and the rocks merged, and although I still had an awareness of being me, I could no longer recognize my body.

Time did not pass in this place like it did when I was on the surface and had a body. I felt that there was still part of me that knew I was trapped, and desperately wanted to be free. As I struggled to understand what was happening, I heard a voice calmly say, "Why struggle, you are fine here. There is nothing that is hurting you. You are safe right where you are." Although I could feel the "Truth" of what this voice was saying, I was indeed safe and nothing was harming me; I also felt that this was not the voice of Oneness, Love or God. This was more like the voice of hopelessness that was telling me to just give up. I somehow understood that living an existence trapped in rock, was not what I desired nor deserved. As I examined my situation and looked for a way out, the voice continued trying to convince me that everything was okay, and that this was my new life, a life without movement, and without purpose.

Unable to find a way to move or to even regain the sense of having a body, I searched my memory of how I had ended up in this place. As I traced my way back down into the depths of the earth and then back into the caverns below, I remembered how I had been brought to those caverns by my guide and could remember having a human form. I became aware that there was still a part of me that was back on the surface, sitting on my couch in meditation. How distant that part of me seemed to be from the me that was experiencing a life trapped in, and being part of solid rock. I wondered if there might be a way for me to contact or communicate with this part of me that was still meditating. I began telling myself that I was that person sitting on the couch, and that I needed to awaken from the meditation. I kept repeating, "Wake up, wake up".

My eyes opened, and I was indeed aware of being in the living room, and back on the surface. I was also keenly aware that I was still far below and trapped in the earth. As I sat there on the couch, I felt my body filled with fear, and shaking as if I were sitting naked in the snow. I tried to relax and tell myself that I was home and safe, but I could not let go of the part of me that was still trapped. It was still early morning, and I didn't want to wake my girlfriend, so I decided to go out back and sit in my spa. Surely the heat of the water would be able stop my shivers.

This entire experience was one of such duality. I was in two places at the same time. I could channel infinite energy, and yet I was totally depleted of energy. I was safe, but completely in fear. Now I was sitting in the hot water of the spa, and yet its heat could not penetrate the cold of the fear. I knew that my guide would never harm me, but here I was no longer feeling like I could trust him. It appeared that opposites could exist at the same time.

After sitting in the spa for awhile and realizing that it was not going to warm me up, I climbed out, dried off, and got dressed. I knew it was time to wake up Tiffany, my girlfriend. She was a gifted psychic and wonderful healer. I knew that she had dealt with dark energies before, and that she would most likely know exactly what to do. I walked into the bedroom, knelt down next to the bed and gently whispered to her that I needed her help. She opened her eyes and turned to look at me. I could see that she had instantly recognized that something was wrong. Her eyes darted from looking at my face, into my eyes and around my energy field. She could see how white my face was, and I know that she was sensing the intense fear that I was feeling. She sat up at the edge of the bed and asked what was going on. I explained the whole story, the meditation, going down into the earth, the caverns, being left by my guide, the creatures, giving my power to help the one poor soul, and getting stuck in the earth.

After Tiffany finished "Reading" my energy and asking me more questions about my experience, she said, "I'm going to need help with this one." She got on the phone, and called two of her closest, psychically gifted friends. She explained the story to both of them, and they came up with a plan. They all agreed that the highest priority problem was that I had given half of my power to one of the creatures. They felt/believed, that by giving that power away, I had surrendered part of my soul, and that they would help facilitate its retrieval. This was my first time hearing about SOUL RETRIEVAL, but it would not be my last.

I was instructed to lie on the floor, flat on my back, and to follow their instructions. The three ladies began by calling on Jesus and all ascended masters for protection. The process of retrieval took more than a half hour, and involved myself and Tiffany following a cord from my physical body, back down into the earth, and to the creature that was in possession of part of my power. The two ladies on the phone held the energy of protection around both Tiffany and me while we were on the journey. Although I had mixed feelings about taking my power away from this dark soul, Tiffany made it quite clear that it needed to be done. The creature reluctantly handed it back to me and we returned back to the living room, and to my body. As the energy was placed back into my heart center, I almost instantly began to feel whole again. I could feel much of the fear dissipate, almost like fine dust being blown off and away into the ether.

Although my power had been returned, and I felt more like the person I had been before the whole experience, I was not myself. I was not the man that I had been before. The memories of the "Hellish" experience were strong, and seemed to strip away so much of my confidence and security. I literally was afraid to be left alone, and the thought of meditating brought only more fear. Tiffany owned a wonderful cat that somehow sensed that I did not want to be alone. The cat spent most of her time with me, sitting on my lap, and offering what comfort she could. This fear went on for weeks before it finally began to dissipate. It would be months before I would meditate again, and even longer before I would trust my guide to take me on another journey.

I had decided early on, in the writing of this book, not to include this episode of my life. I believed that it had too many negative components, and that I would not be able to adequately relate the intensity of its effect on my life; yet I also have to admit, that although it had brought up such intense fear, it had also been perhaps one of the most profound, and beneficial meditations I have ever experienced. As I have stated numerous times, Truth is only what is being viewed from the particular place that you are standing, and can never include anything in its entirety.

When I view this meditation from a place of fear, I see the caverns, the creatures and the solidity of the earth as real physical manifestations. From this lens or filter of fear, I interpret reality as happening all around me, to me and sometimes against me. I believe that the reality around me has power over me, and that I can actually become helpless when faced with such overwhelming forces. In the movie "The Matrix," there is a point where Neo is PRACTICE fighting against Morpheus, in a virtual simulation. In the beginning Neo is full of energy and confidence, but as the battle progresses, Neo becomes exhausted and is barely able to catch his breath. Morpheus looks at him and asks if he really believes that he is tired or if he thinks that he is really breathing air? After all, this is only a simulation, taking place in the mind. With that reminder, Neo is able to regain his composure, his strength and his confidence. He has been reminded that REALITY is only ever seen from where you are standing, and with this new view of what is real, he is not and cannot be overwhelmed.

It has been more than twenty years since this meditation, and even to this day I keep having new revelations regarding it. It is as though the experience planted seeds for an entire garden, and new flowers bloom each time I am reminded of the meditation. My life has brought me to many different places to stand, and places to view the meditation from. There have been points where I suddenly understood that anytime I would feel "Stuck" in life, it was similar to being stuck in the earth, and unable to move upward; that being stuck was in a way like being in Hell. Hell did not need to be a place of great suffering; when I was stuck in the solidity of the earth, I was not suffering. There was no physical pain. I was not being tortured emotionally, nor was I being threatened in any way. In fact, there was only this calm voice telling me that there was no need to struggle; that I was safe and okay. But life without movement, without the flow of change, is no life at all. We can and often do create our lives in a way where we feel safe and secure and yet have very little movement forward. We might even feel that by creating such a safe predictable life, we have become successful, that we have conquered life and its challenges. Yet what we have really accomplished, is making a cozy spot where we can be unaffected by the flow of life. We have given up our freedom, and the infinite possibilities that life has to offer, for the illusion of safety.

As I look back at the meditation through the filter of "Gratitude", I am forever counting the blessings that have been brought into my life from this amazing experience. It has been a wonderful gift to recognize, when and how, I would "Give up" on life, and resign myself to a life that was not moving forward, that did not include passion or adventure. From this place of Gratitude, what might have once appeared to be an insurmountable problem, can now be seen as an opportunity or even a gift to experience life in a different way.

When looking at any problem through the lens of fear, we feel small, helpless and insignificant. When looking at the very same problem through the lens of gratitude, we recognize that the "Problem" only exists for our benefit. It is always there to give us the opportunity to view and live life in a greater way. How we choose to view life is the most important aspect of being aware. Life is always about where we are "Standing." During the meditation, I was standing in a place where the caverns and the creatures were physically REAL. My experience of intense fear was REAL. Upon waking in my body, back on the couch, I was standing in a place where both the caverns, creatures and my waking life were REAL. Now, so many years later, I am standing in a place where I see that any "Reality" is only REAL based on where we are standing; this includes even our waking reality.

Before ending this story, I would like to address the idea of "Soul Retrieval." As with all definitions, there will be people that see it a different way than how I will be explaining it. This is only my interpretation, or view of my experience, and understanding of the term. I don't believe it is even possible to lose a part of your soul, but it is my experience that parts of the soul can be abandoned or hidden in the deepest recesses of our being.

I believe that it is most often during, or after, experiencing great emotional trauma, that we seem to "Lose," or block off, a part of ourselves. This emotional trauma may be partly attributed to a physical trauma, but I believe that it is generally because of the intense emotions involved that we feel like some part of us has been stripped away. People that have experienced PTSD, are a good example of how trauma has changed how a person feels and behaves. They see or view life from a more limited perspective. Those that have, or are experiencing PTSD, recognize that many of the upper levels of consciousness (Gratitude, Joy, Love and Peace) no longer seem to be accessible. It is as though the part of the self that was able to experience these emotions or levels of being, has somehow disappeared. It could be said or viewed that a part of the soul is missing.

This experience or feeling that a part of the self is gone can happen when a child is severely abused, or when a soldier sees more than they can deal with, or when we experience a great loss. There are many experiences that can be so emotionally traumatic that our minds just can't seem to handle them. In such cases we may abandon or close off a part of ourselves. When this happens, we no longer feel whole. We no longer function, or interact with the world in the same way. It is not a conscious choice to close off a part of ourselves, it is more like that part is just too painful to access.

I am sure that there are plenty of clinical terms for what I am describing, and I am sure that there are clinical treatments that would attempt to deal with these situations, but from my personal experience with "Soul Loss," re-incorporating the abandoned part with the whole, would be unique with each person. There are people that have been trained in different techniques for "Soul Retrieval." It would seem reasonable that a certain technique may work better for one person, while a different technique would be better in another case. Over the years, I have been involved, or helped with many retrievals. Each one was quite unique, and some seemed extraordinary. It has also been my experience, and understanding, that Ayahuasca can be of benefit in reuniting parts of the soul.

It is my belief that most people have, at some point in their life, gone through a trauma that has caused them to abandon, or close off a part of their being. It would not be uncommon for someone to close off many parts or aspects of themselves as they go through one trauma after another. Western medicine may have different drugs to treat such people, but if given the choice, I for one would make "Soul Retrieval "an option.

When I was between the ages of eight and fifteen, I had many dreams where I had been in a fight with someone and ended up killing them. I would search hard for a place to hide or bury the body, but in every case, I knew that the body would eventually be found, and that people would know that I was the one responsible. These dreams bothered me a great deal. I was not a violent young man, and never really thought about killing anyone. It would be years before I would understand that each of the battles that I had fought, and each of the bodies that I buried, were not other people, but rather they were parts of myself that I was trying to hide. They were the parts that didn't "Fit in" with who others thought I should be. I tried to abandon them, kill them, hide them, but always knew that someday they would be discovered.

It was only recently that I thought to meditate, and ask what these parts were, that I had felt so compelled to hide. I wondered if these were aspects of myself that still lay hidden in the recesses of my soul; or had they somehow been reincorporated as I grew up and became a man. I sat back and slipped easily into a deep meditative state. I could sense that not only was my guide present, but that he was already aware of my question, and all too happy to reveal the answer. We sailed off into the oneness of all existence, to the place that would seem to be where I was before coming into this earthly life. In this PLACE, there was such a sense of unconditional love. Every being seemed to radiate this love, almost as though it was the actual core of each being. There is no love on earth that comes close to the penetrating love that is experienced on the other side of the veil. My guide showed me how it is necessary to forget this love, to create barriers to block the feeling and the remembering of this infinite love, in order to enter the world of the physical. I could see and understand the necessity for this forgetting; we could not do or be what we have come here for, if we recognized who we truly are, and where we actually come from.

My guide showed me how even as a child, I somehow knew or expected that I should be loved unconditionally by everyone! Even though I could not consciously remember where I came from, I somehow still felt this unity, and had a difficult time understanding that being loved by others came with judgments, as though love needed to be earned or deserved. Each person seemed to have different expectations of me, and if I wanted their love, I needed to behave in a particular way. The parts of me that did not fit into what others expected of me needed to be hidden, and not expressed.

Some of those parts did not want to be abandoned, and in my dreams, I would have to battle them, overcome them, and hide them. Each time I would hide one of these parts or bodies, I always knew that at some point, they would be discovered, and that everyone would know what I had done, and who I truly was.

Who knows how many parts of ourselves we have abandoned and hidden away? How can we ever be whole, when so much is missing?

Story #16-Resistance

I had been a handyman for several years, working by myself helping people with almost any type of project that they needed done. Most of the time it was a "learn as you go" scenario for me. I was painting, building fences and decks, patching drywall, repairing minor plumbing and electrical problems and just about anything that someone would ask me to do. Then in 1989 I became a licensed General Contractor. I was still doing all the same things I did as a handyman, but now I could charge more and legally take on larger projects.

I had already developed a large client base, and no longer needed to advertise. In fact, I went the next seventeen years without advertising. Back then, most advertising was done with fliers, newspapers, and in the phone book; no such thing as the internet or social media back then. Most of my clients were Realtors, Property Managers or Investors, and all were repeat customers, keeping me and my small crew as busy as I could handle. Working with people this way allowed me to actually develop close relationships with my clients, and I enjoyed having a great reputation.

As easy as this sounds, I really did take my responsibility as a Contractor seriously. I wanted every one of my jobs to go well, and for each of my clients to be happy with the work that we did. If you have ever watched a home improvement show, then you know that every project comes with unexpected problems. You open a wall and find improper wiring, or that a pipe has been leaking for years and caused major damage. The problem could be termites or that the previous owner had done work himself and didn't really know what he was doing. I have replaced hundreds of garbage disposals, and yet each time there is something that makes each job unique.

Besides the actual work having its challenges, there were other factors in being a licensed Contractor. Everybody wanted a "cut" of my business. The State wanted its license fees and required multiple types of insurance from a Bond to Liability to Worker Compensation, and sometimes a Performance Bond. I was required to obtain a license in every city or county that I would do work in. Then there were city and county permits, and they often required building plans to be submitted. Along with everything else, there was employee payroll and taxes that needed to be paid. I was also required to pay quarterly taxes on my business. There became so much paperwork to do to keep the business going that I had little time to actually be on a job site. This made it more difficult for me to be assured that the quality of the work that I expected was getting done.

The point that I am trying to make, is that with each requirement there was another layer of stress added. When I was a handyman, I would quote a job, do the job and get paid. Being a Contractor was a whole new world. It would be years before I would understand the damage that stress was doing on my life. There was the physical stress from pounding nails, to crawling in attics, and sub-areas, to working on roofs or the constant looking up, working on ceilings. There was heavy lifting and working for long periods in such awkward positions. All of this put a strain on my physical body that made weekly visits to a chiropractor necessary. I also began to take pain medication daily and then still often needed to use ice packs, heating pads and daily stretching. Then there was the emotional stress, worrying about every job, working eighty hours a week, and not having enough time to spend with my wife and children.

Eventually I understood that the requirements to maintain my business were more than I was willing to pay. I know that I needed to stop being a Contractor! What I didn't understand at the time, was how we get "Programmed from Life." As difficult as my contracting business had become, I had programmed myself to live the life of a contractor. Through repetition, doing the same thing every day, I had become a contractor in my mind. My thoughts were about the business, and everything that it required of me. My clients that I had developed relationships with had expectations of me. My crew relied on me to provide work and income for them. My family relied on me to provide the financial support that kept the bills paid and food on the table.

I had developed a huge resistance to continuing the business, and at the same time there were so many reasons to resist walking away from it. Resistance is just a word, and it's funny how many different meanings that it has. It could mean not wanting to do a particular thing. Medically it could mean having a resistance to something like a virus. Electrically it means opposing the flow of an electrical current. Biologically it means, building a resistance to a medication or even to a toxin. In Physics it would be like how the resistance in the air, limits the speed we can travel. For me, resistance means all of the above.

As I pondered what resistance felt like for me, I knew that although there was a part of me that really enjoyed being a contractor, that enjoyed interacting with my clients, and figuring out how to make repairs or alterations, there was a larger, more "knowing" part that knew it was time to make a change. As with the medical definition of resistance, life had caused me to build resistance to the problems of contracting. I had learned to live with the physical and emotional challenges that this career came with. I was able to go through day-to-day life and get things done.

Now as I look at the Electrical definition of resistance I am hit with the deeper reality of living as a physical being. I understand that every cell in my body carries an electrical current. I can see how resistance to any part of life, means resistance to the current in those very cells. Stress can often be used as another word for resistance, and stress was literally creating havoc at the cellular level. If the cells can't function correctly or communicate properly, the body suffers.

It is easy to understand that stress can cause a headache, or neck pain, or even an ulcer, so it only makes sense that we can carry that stress in any part of our body. While stress may cause a headache in a short time; that same amount of stress held in the gut may take years to manifest into an ulcer. Would there be any limit to the type of problem that stress or resistance could cause? Could it be that resistance could be a huge contributing factor in just about any human ailment?

Biologically, resistance would be like building a resistance to medications, or to the things that we would be doing to alleviate our suffering. We might need to take stronger medications or start other types of treatments in order to maintain the same level of physical activity. In my case, I needed to use ice packs on my neck and back more often. I had become accustomed to taking pain medications multiple times a day. I had purchased different massage units that I would use daily. I was sleeping with magnets on the areas that were more painful. I could only sleep with my body in certain positions. I had adapted my life to the "fact" that continuing the business of contracting, meant my body would require more and more intervention to keep it going, and it was becoming more resistant to each type of treatment that I provided it.

Resistance in Physics could be looked at or described as "friction." The friction in the air limits the speed we can travel. The friction of water is even greater than air, limiting movement even further. Walking through deep snow can quickly zap strength from the body. I could see how living my life as a contractor had caused me to build resistance to moving forward. In the beginning there was an excitement about taking on a job, and there was the financial reward to look forward to. Now, decades later, the excitement had faded away, and the financial rewards no longer seemed so important. I had become programmed to life as a contractor, but every day I could feel the denseness of moving through the motions of my business. Even though each aspect of the business, from understanding a job, to calculating the estimate, to knowing what tools to use or how to interact with my clients, had become so intellectually easy, they had also become emotionally difficult. I would have to force myself to sit at the computer and write up an estimate, and even as I would finish a job, it might take me days before I could again force myself to sit and write out the bill for that job.

In April of 2020 my wife passed after a long battle with cancer. A few months later I sold a "fixer" property that I had purchased with a wonderful business partner. With the sale of the property, I was able to pay off all of my debts, and knew that it was finally time for me to retire. With the loss of my wife, much of life had lost its luster, and I knew that I needed to move forward into something different. I told all of my long-term clients that I was closing my business, and that I could refer them to another contractor. As it turned out, I had decided to retire just when contractors were needed the most.

In the past year and a half, the world, my country, my state, my town and myself had gone through an unprecedented amount of turmoil. First there had been the beginning of the

"Pandemic," an event that seemed to have changed the world, down to how each of us behaved in everyday life. The U.S. went through the most unusual presidential election of my lifetime, leaving the country more divided than it had been since the Civil War. It literally separated families by political parties. Conspiracy theories began to proliferate to the point where so much of the country felt that they could no longer trust the mainstream news, or even our own election system. QAnon and other wild stories were given birth, dividing the country in the most unusual ways. Reality itself was viewed from such extreme viewpoints. My beautiful wife transitioned from this physical life, leaving me in such a state of grief. California was experiencing the worst drought in history, leaving millions of trees dead or dying, and the reservoirs at dangerously low levels. In 2020, California experienced the worst fire season on record, and the largest single fire in the state's history had stopped just short of where I live; in fact I had been under an evacuation order. The smoke had been so thick that for days and days it had blocked the sun, so that the middle of the day looked like the middle of the night. The loss of so much animal habitat due to the drought and the fires had changed animal behaviors. Bears had always been a part of living in my town, and I lived right on a creek that backed up to a National Forest. Bears would come by almost every night, but after the fires I would have multiple bears wandering by during the middle of the day, skinny and hungry. In 2021 California once again set new records for the most fires, the most land burned and the largest single fire. Near Yosemite, where I live, and the surrounding areas were hit with the strongest windstorm on record, with clocked winds over 120 mph, leaving so many homes and areas without electrical service, and trees lying on the tops of home after home. Most homes received their water supply from their individual wells, and the loss of electricity meant the loss of their water also. So many homes had been damaged from the winds and falling trees, that within two days, there was not a roll of plastic or a tarp to be found in my little town. For years the population of wild turkeys had been growing, and they would roost every night in the tops of the tallest pine trees. It was amazing to watch these giant birds lift from the ground like helicopters going almost straight up to the tops of the trees, and then every morning they would use my driveway as a landing pad to return to earth. After the windstorm I was left with approximately 10 percent of the number of turkeys that I had before the storm. In 2021 my town and the surrounding areas experienced the hottest summer on record, giving another blow to the wildlife, and the loss of habitat, and water supply. Also, in 2021 much of California was hit with what had been called an "atmospheric river," the heaviest rainfall on record. 2020 and 2021 also brought record supply shortages to the entire U.S. from paper goods, computer chips, lumber, building materials and just about everything else.

It's hard to imagine that so many record setting events took place in just these two years, but what it meant for the contracting business was nothing short of a boon. So many houses had been lost or damaged from the fires. So many homes in my area had been left severely damaged from the windstorm, and even some of my very best friends were unable to find an available contractor to help them. All this was combined with the Covid Pandemic, allowing for so many more people to work from home, creating a greater call for the remodeling of those homes. Every contractor had increased their rates for both materials and labor, and even with these higher rates they could not keep up with demand. In all my years as a contractor I had never seen such a need for my service, and yet here I was trying to retire, just when I seemed to be needed the most.

I was excited about retiring because I had so many projects that had been left on the back burners, things that I really wanted to pursue, but just didn't have the time for. This book for one, was calling me with such intensity. I have a sawmill and lots of dead trees around that are just asking to be made into furniture or art projects. I have fun ideas regarding a line of clothing along with other ideas that just seem like they could be so much fun to create.

As much as I was looking forward to retiring, and having the time to pursue these other projects, my phone would not stop ringing, old clients, newer clients, friends, people who had heard about me, everybody looking for a contractor. Most of them I would give out the names and numbers for other contractors, but some that I knew quite well, had already called every contractor around, and were now asking me for help. I continued taking on one job after another, and it seemed there was no end in sight.

Then one night I had a very powerful dream. I was standing in a room with several people that I knew to be my friends. The one standing closest to me was holding a baseball bat, and I knew that he was going to hit me in the head with it. I willingly prepared myself to get hit. I adjusted my stance in order to stand as solidly as possible and then said, "Go ahead and hit me." My friend took a powerful swing, and the bat struck me on the left side of my head. Immediately I could feel the pain, and I could feel the swelling begin. I fell to the floor as both the swelling and the pain intensified. As I lie there I pondered whether I would even survive this hit, and if I did survive, would I even want to? I knew that the blow had caused such damage that I would never be the same, I would never be able to fully heal.

It was at this point that I awoke from the dream. I knew that this was not just an ordinary dream; it was sending me a message. To say that I was concerned would be an understatement. There was such an intensity, almost an anguish over what I had just experienced. I wasted no time. I climbed out of bed and headed right to my spot on the couch, where I would meditate nearly every day. It took only moments for me to get comfortable and reach out to my guide. I didn't even need to formulate the question, before he was showing me my answer. It was so simple and so obvious; I was allowing my friends to hit me with one more job!

OMG! I had built up so much resistance to working as a contractor, and at the same time I was resisting ending the business. Each of these ideas was held firmly in place by thoughts and emotions. There were so many reasons to continue helping my friends, and these reasons were shored up with emotions of friendship, loyalty, love and responsibility. The reasons for ending the business were supported with the emotions of freedom, love for myself and the excitement for a new life. Now the dream was making it clear that this duality was killing me. For the first time I was able to understand the significance of saying good-bye to my contracting business. I was finally ready to let it go. As I write this story it has been less than a week since I finished my last job as a contractor.

If you are human, then your life is probably full of resistance. We might have resistance to our job, our parents, our children, to politics, to a love relationship, to healthy eating, to exercising and to just about anything. Resistance by its very nature causes turmoil in the body and mind, but in my case I had resistance to keeping my business and resistance to letting it go, then there is double the resistance and it seemed to be a no win situation. Many people seem to stay in a relationship that they know is not good for them, and I have been guilty of judging these people, thinking how silly it is to stay where you don't want to be, and yet that is exactly what I had been doing with my business. It's much easier to see someone else's problems, because we are not caught up in all the thoughts and emotions of those problems.

Another way of looking at resistance is to recognize that it is how we say "No" to Life! We are saying no to what's happening, and that is the same as saying no to life. For me, I was saying no to keeping my business, and saying no to letting the business go. Staying in this situation had been creating turmoil in my mind, keeping me emotionally on edge, and causing pain in my body. Part of me believed that if I could just embrace my business, and work with joy then all would be well. I believed that the pains in my body would heal, and that the turmoil in my life would go away. Yet a larger part of me knew that I was done with this work, and that I had so much more to offer the world, and the world had so much more to offer me.

As I have pondered this thing called resistance, it seems that it's full of judgments. It's difficult sometimes to determine the difference between a judgment and an awareness. A judgment is a point of view, where as awareness would be more like the actual recognition or truth of a thing. There is clarity in awareness that does not exist with judgments and points of view. There is a knowing that just does not carry resistance with it. If we could somehow be able to determine whether we are looking at a situation with clarity, and without judgments, then life would be so much easier. Resistance would disappear or at least lose most of its intensity.

It has been said that resistance is the cause of all suffering, and yet by recognizing that things could be different, we often find the motivation to seek another path. I believe that the problem arises when we resist what is, and yet we choose to maintain the situation and the resistance to it. There are times when it is appropriate to let go of the resistance, and to change how we see the situation. There are times that we need to change the situation in order to end the resistance. Unfortunately, we all too often decide to continue with both the situation and our resistance to it. Maintaining the resistance is the cause of suffering, and it creates turmoil in the mind and body. This turmoil can eventually manifest in physical pain, disease or in some type of emotional problem, such as anxiety or depression. RESISTANCE is life giving us a message that we need to change our point of view, or we need to change the situation. Are we listening to Life?

Story #17-The Quantum Self

For as long as I can remember, I have been fascinated by how things work. Science has perhaps shaped our view of reality as much as religion, parents, teachers or even our own perceptions. Science has tried to explain the universe, our planet, nature and its laws, how we were created, and what keeps us alive. For all of our technology, and great scientific minds, it is amazing how many of science's explanations are still based on theory. You take away the beginning theory or premise, and the explanation falls apart.

I have been very interested in what being human means. Some of the latest science has explained human development in amazing detail. The field of Quantum Physics has opened incredible views of the formation of life. I have always enjoyed statistics, feeling that they were a good method of putting things in perspective. I would like to take this opportunity to share a few of the statistics that seem almost mind blowing, concerning human development.

First, according to science, everything is made up of atoms. Atoms are the building blocks that form the Earth, the sky, a tree, a turtle or a person. We were all taught about atoms in school, but the description of atoms has changed over time. Science tells us that an atom is 99.9999999% space and energy, and that only the neutrons, protons and electrons are actually particles. Quantum Mechanics now says that these "particles" are incredibly small and that they blink in and out of existence. The atom is not always here, it pops into reality, and then disappears. In fact, some scientists say that atoms only have a tendency to exist. Some of the newer theories say that even electrons, protons and neutrons are spinning vortexes of energy and not actually particles. If the only particles that make up matter are not really particles, and they blink in and out of existence, then what is matter? To this date, no science has ever found or proven the existence of a particle. There is a very good possibility that there is NO MATTER in what we call matter!

If an atom is more than 99.9% space and energy and the supposedly solid parts make up such a small fraction of the atom, why are we so concerned about the solid parts? Why do we ignore the space and energy parts of the equation? Just like we don't really understand electrons, protons and neutrons, we also don't understand space and energy. We talk about energy like we know all about it, but even though it's everywhere we really don't know where it comes from or how it exists.

According to the Periodic Table, there are roughly one hundred and nine types of atoms. Each type of atom represents an element. The difference in what makes the element Oxygen instead of the element Potassium is how many protons the atoms contain. Still each element is made up of atoms. Out of the roughly one hundred nine different elements, only eleven are needed to create a human being. Out of those eleven elements, six make up roughly ninety nine percent of a body, leaving the remaining five elements to make up less than one percent.

So, what does it take to make a human? Before being fertilized, a human egg is made up of only one cell. According to science, there are roughly 100 TRILLION atoms in a single cell! These are not just any old atoms, they need to be the exact type and number of atoms required to form a human cell. That single egg needs to be made of the right number of Oxygen atoms and carbon atoms and hydrogen atoms and so on. Those atoms have to be held together in just the right sequence, bonded together to form an actual living, working, functioning cell!

We have been told that all the information needed to make a human is found in the DNA. I would like to point out that DNA, like everything else in our "reality," is made up entirely of atoms! This means that atoms somehow must know how to form DNA. It takes over two billion atoms to form a strand of DNA, with each cell having its own strand. If DNA holds the information to create a human, and that DNA is made of atoms, how do the atoms know how to create the DNA? Atoms, being made of energy, space, neutrons, protons and electrons, somehow come together to form molecules and structures like DNA. But still, the atom is the foundation of all structures. So where in the atoms that form DNA, is the information on how to create a human? Is the information in the electrons? Is the information in the space? Perhaps it is in the energy. How is it possible that by atoms bonding together in huge numbers, that suddenly information is created? Not only information magically appears, but so does LIFE! According to science, atoms bond together to form molecules and sometimes compounds and what suddenly makes atoms turn into life, is the chemical processes that take place. In fact, according to science, there are approximately thirty-seven billion, billion chemical reactions every second in a human body.

The average length of a human pregnancy is two hundred and eighty days. Estimates range from 26 billion to 2 trillion cells that make up an average human baby at birth, each cell containing one hundred trillion atoms. From the original single cell egg, cell division begins. One cell divides into two and those two divide into four and so on. It is said that these cells go through forty-one divisions in the creation of a completed body. The human body contains over two hundred types of cells, a liver cell being different than a skin cell or a blood cell etc. The DNA therefore not only has to provide the information as to what type of cell is being created, but also the location that each cell must be in. You wouldn't want the eye cells showing up at the tip of a finger. A cell is not an inanimate object, it is a living, functioning cell with a job to do. There is no training needed, the cell begins its functions immediately upon being created. So even if we somehow discover where the information comes from to build a cell, where is the information that the cell needs in order to know what its function is?

Due to the process of cell division, at the beginning, progress is slow with small numbers of cells being formed, and in the last few weeks, an enormous amount of cells are created. Just as a reference, if we used the figure of 2 trillion cells in an average baby[iii], and averaged the creation of cells equally over the two hundred and eighty days of pregnancy, the mother would have to make eighty-three thousand cells per second! Each of these cells being made up of 100 trillion atoms, all in the proper ratios as to the parts they are making, some atoms becoming cell lining, some becoming the fluid inside the cell, some becoming parts of the mitochondria, etc. This would totally put to shame any projects that man has ever created, from skyscrapers to rockets or monster dams.

With over seven billion people on the planet, we are certainly used to babies being born, but as we look at what it actually takes to create one of these wondrous miniature earthlings, we have to be stunned by the magic involved. If everything is made of atoms, where is the information stored to create the DNA? It can't be stored in DNA which is only created after the atoms form it. Regardless, creating a physical being from using the same building blocks that create stars is beyond comprehension. Yet, this is what we have been taught, and for the most part, it is what we have believed.

As I said in the beginning, science needs to rely on theories, and a beginning premise in order for their explanation to work. One of those basic premises is that "Matter" exists. We have been taught that matter is solid and that it forms everything we see. We see it, touch it, stand on it, pick it up and hold it, make artwork from it, make cars and airplanes out of it. We make structures that we work in and live in out of it, so it would surely seem natural to conclude that it is real and exists. Yet if science has not been able to establish or prove the existence of one particle of matter, perhaps we might want to open our minds to greater possibilities. If indeed matter is not solid, and by the way, that would also mean that we are not solid either, then what is matter and what are we?

Are we the "Quantum Self," made from atoms that have an extremely sketchy existence? Are we made of energy that we don't really understand? If we don't understand matter or energy, what are the chances that we somehow can rely on our understanding of the third part of the atom, space to be accurate? Does space exist anything like how we perceive it? The more we look at "reality" the more we understand how little we know of it. All we can have is a point of view and by definition all points of view are limited. It seems crazy how hard we as people will fight to defend our point of view, instead of opening our minds to greater possibilities.

If we were to be having a dream and in that dream we are looking at a table, and then the thought pops into our head, "I wonder what this table is made of," we might design something like a microscope to look at the structure of the table. Looking through this microscope, we would see that the wood table is made of fibers. We might then ask what the fibers are made from? We might make a stronger microscope that allows us to peer deeper into the structure. As we look deeper and deeper, what had seemed to be solid wood, becomes less solid, with any visible structure disappearing. We might develop ideas of molecules forming the structure of wood. Then we ask, what are molecules made from? We develop the ideas of smaller particles that we call atoms. Yes, we think that atoms are the building blocks that make solid objects. We can't see these atoms, but we know that something has to exist to explain how we can perceive this piece of wood as a table. Then we ask what atoms are made from, and we come up with the idea of protons, neutrons and electrons. Then just as always seems to happen, we ask," What are these parts of the atoms made from?"

The deeper we look into what makes up any object, the farther down the rabbit hole we go. How far down this hole do we travel until we understand that this is a dream and there is no solidity to any object? Even the microscope is as much a part of the dream as is any piece of equipment that we can conceive. In fact, we are no more solid than the table or the microscope, we are as much a part of the dream as anything else. So, the real, true question is, WHO is doing the dreaming?

Story #18-What is everything made of

For the purpose of this discussion, when referring to "everything" I am speaking of what we call the physical universe. This includes everything from atoms, energy, living creatures, planets, stars and even our very thoughts. This includes all things related to our physical experience. Since we see light and hear sound, these must all be included in our experience of reality. Even how and what we feel are part of our reality and therefore must be included in the "everything."

As it is with everyone else, all that I can have is a point of view. So what follows can only be from a certain point of view, and cannot contain the entire truth. I don't believe that it is possible for anyone, while in physical form to know or experience the entire truth of anything. While some points of view are quite limiting, some can be far more expanding. During my Ayahuasca ceremonies, and my deepest most profound meditations, I feel that I have had the opportunities to experience and understand physical reality from a much larger perspective. Most of my times experiencing expanded awareness have been described by or are similar to those experienced by mystics throughout the ages.

Many mystics and masters have described what we know as physical reality, to be nothing more than a dream. If this is indeed a dream, then who is doing the dreaming, and for what purpose? Is there only one dreamer or hundreds or millions of dreamers? If this is a dream, then what is everything made of, and is any of it actually real? There are those that have described reality as only being "real" according to where you are standing. While in a dream, the character in the dream sees all of it as real, and yet upon awakening, it becomes apparent that the character and every part of the dream had somehow been manufactured by the dreamer. From the awakened dreamer's perspective, This reality now seems to be real, but what if a higher perspective is possible? While in deep meditation or in my Ayahuasca experiences, I absolutely reached states of being where I seemed to be looking back on this physical life as a dream, and while in that higher state, it felt more real than this physical reality. As we change where we stand and where we see reality from, reality literally changes.

I had previously discussed that while in this physical world, we can only know a small fraction of the truth of anything. According to some scientists, we are constantly showered with a massive amount of information and yet we are only aware of a tiny fraction of that information. Some scientists have suggested that we are hit with as much as four hundred billion bits of information every second, and yet we only process about two thousand of those bits. That means for every single bit of information that we are aware of, there are another two hundred million bits that we are not conscious of. We feel that as we look out into the world, we are seeing the totality of it, and that we understand what we are seeing; yet this is far from the truth. The extremely small percentage of the information that we process is going to be the parts that fit into our "points of view" about life. How can we ever have a greater understanding or "transformation," if we continually ignore so much information, and pay attention only to the things that fit into our small box of reality?"

As an example, we have all become used to seeing our own reflection in a mirror, but what are we actually looking at? According to the dictionary, Reflection is "the bending or folding back of light or sound waves from a surface." Just like we really don't know what Matter is, we also don't really know what light and sound are either. We talk about sound and light being frequencies, and that implies that *something* must be vibrating in order to create a frequency. If we have not been able to establish that *matter* exists, then *what* is vibrating? My point here is that we simply take for granted that we understand what we see and hear. We look in the mirror and assume that we are seeing a flesh and blood, solid, absolutely real human being. We think we are seeing a true reflection of who we are. In a dream, if you looked into a mirror, you would most likely see yourself reflected back. Is there something that is vibrating in the dream that would create that reflection of you, or are both you and your reflection created by Consciousness itself? Yet this reflection is a shadow of our true being. We have ignored the greater information, in favor of the information that fits into our view of who we think we are.

In the case of looking at your reflection in a mirror, we have to ask what that reflection is made out of. In fact, what are you made of, what is the mirror made of, and what is anything made out of? When looking at your reflection, are you looking at matter? If you can look at a face and see more than just the matter that seems to be what the face is made out of, for instance is this face angry or happy or friendly, then what are you really seeing? Is looking at a face more than just seeing it, is it more of an experience? Somehow there is information being transferred from the face in the mirror to you, and then being deciphered, put through your life filters, and then registered as your perception.

As we discussed earlier, there is a very real possibility that matter has no existence of its own. There is most likely no matter in matter. What if there is no energy in energy, no space in space and no time in time? What if everything that we experience in this "physical" world is made from INFORMATION! What if we are simply deciphering and filtering information and that becomes our unique way of perceiving the entire universe?

If we were again to look at a dream, it makes sense that everything in that dream is coming from our imagination, and represents nothing more than thoughts and perhaps emotions. What seems to be a solid building made out of matter, is only being perceived as solid by the dreamed self; for the dreamer, it becomes quite obvious upon awakening, that there never was any matter or space involved in the dream, yet there had been a "reality" about the dreamed experience. Since the dream was actually experienced, then what was it made out of? We could say that the entire dream had been made out of thoughts, but thoughts are "something." That "something" could also be described as information. The entire dream, including the dreamed self, was made from "filtered" bits of information, that we call thoughts.

According to Neuroscience, thoughts are produced by electrochemical reactions that occur when impulses are transmitted across synapses between nerve cells in the brain. This sounds very scientific, but the brain and the nerve cells are both made out of matter, something that science has not been able to prove the existence of. How those impulses are transformed into thoughts is also very much debatable. As with so much of our physical existence, science has many theories, but very little actual, provable facts. Perhaps the only thing that we as humans might all agree on, is that we are "Aware." While in a dream, we as a dreamed character are aware of our surroundings and that we somehow seem to have an existence. As a human in the waking state, we are aware of our surroundings, and that we somehow seem to exist. Being aware would appear to be the one truth that we all share. So what if all of our physical perception is just the deciphering and filtering of information?

As an example, science tells us that colors do not actually exist. Instead, colors are our way of processing certain types of information. Many creatures and many humans are what we refer to as "color blind," they do not process information into colors. For them, colors do not exist. Then there are many people that can actually feel colors, and some that have described being able to hear colors audibly. I have watched as different colored papers were set on a table, and then a sheet of glass placed over them. I watched as someone who was blindfolded would hold their hand over each piece of paper and describe the color of the paper. The point here is that whatever bits of information that make up what we call colors, can be perceived into awareness from what would seem to be different senses. Colors are more than what we see with our eyes, they are bits or perhaps waves of information, and we have chosen to describe this type of information as color.

Just as with the example of color, sounds could also be described as information. We have all heard the question "If a tree falls in the forest and no one is around to hear it, does it make a sound?" Without a "perceiver" there would indeed be no sound. There would be information such as vibrations in the air, but without a perceiver to interpret those vibrations into sound, the falling tree would only send out information and not actually sound. What we call sound is only the way that we have chosen to describe a type of information.

The same is true for all of our senses. The sense of touch is only the way that we interpret information. When our fingers touch a drinking glass, information is brought into awareness. Keep in mind that our fingers are made of matter and the electrical impulses that touching the glass produces are sent through nerves that are made of matter to a brain that is made of matter. Those impulses are then sent through synapses and somehow interpreted into the feeling of touching a glass. While from our seemingly physical perspective, the transfer of impulses through nerves and interpreted into touch appears to be real; perhaps it is only real from this very localized perspective, just like a dream seems to be real from the dreamed character's perspective. Let's not forget that matter may not actually exist, at least not in the way that we believe it does. The fingers, the nerves, the brain, the synapses and even the impulses, are all part of this perceived reality, and may only appear real from a localized perspective.

What if every atom that appears to be what your body is constructed of, is instead just information, and not matter? What if everything that we perceive in this physical world is just how "Awareness" perceives information? If everything that we perceive is in fact information, we are still left with questions like where is the information coming from, and for what purpose? Looking back at the scenario of dreaming, it seems very plausible that the entire dream could be information being noticed or watched through the eyes of awareness. It would seem upon awakening that it was the dreamer that was responsible for the information being experienced in the dream. Many of us have experienced having a dream in a dream. We wake up and realize that we were dreaming and believe that we are now awake, only to wake from that dream into this supposed reality. From each place that we stand, our perception tells us that our experience is real. It is not until we change where we are standing that we become aware that we had only been dreaming. Reality is literally in the eye of the beholder.

When we dream, it is easy to understand that everything in the dream was somehow created by us, the dreamer. The dream did not come from outside of us, it was created by our thoughts and emotions, which we could describe as information. We created the dream, and we also perceived the dream. The dreamer and the dream are inseparable. The information and the perceiver of the information are one in the same.

In this "Reality" that we perceive as real and happening all around us, we are again perceiving information that has taken the form of an outside world. This world appears separate from us, yet our perception of the world changes as we change our point of view of how we see it. In a dream, we have all had the experience of perceiving the dream from the viewpoint of the dreamed character that we identify as us, but we have also experienced the dream from "Outside" of that dreamed character; sometimes seeing the dream unfold from above, like we are watching a movie. Sometimes we experience the dream not only from the main character's point of view, but sometimes from the perspective of other characters or animals in the dream, even feeling their thoughts and emotions. It is as though experience is subject to where the attention of "Awareness" is placed or focused.

Those that have experienced hallucinatory drugs or adventures with Ayahuasca, may be aware that just like in a dream, they did not actually go anywhere in order to experience these levels of awareness. Instead, awareness is shifted into realms that are not generally accessed by our conscious mind. We may have the most profound experiences of expanded consciousness and travel in thought to viewing points that allow us to see and experience life in new ways. When a medium is able to access information from those that have crossed over, they did not go anywhere to be able to access that information, instead they opened a door to view information from a different point of awareness. The same is true for psychics, artists and even great thinkers.

ALL of the information is around us or accessible to us at any point. Any one of us has the capability to access feeling colors, or communicating with animals, or seeing angels around us. Every way of viewing "reality" is available to each of us. It does seem, however, that we as humans each believe that how we see life, and realty is the correct way of perceiving it. We often take pride in sharing our perspective on just about any subject, believing that this perspective is the one and only way of perceiving this subject. In each case the view is correct, but only from that specific place of understanding. Even in the science of physics, scientists are seeing that when they change how they see an event, the event actually changes. How we see everything changes everything that we see. This is indeed the most powerful secret of life that has always been in plain sight for us to witness. This is the secret of "Transformation." We have the ability to change everything around us, including ourselves! This is the most profound message shared by the Masters throughout the ages. When you see someone as your enemy, then that is who and what they are to you. When you see that same person through the eyes of Mother Teresa, you see that person as Jesus in one of his many disguises. Changing how you see a thing, changes that thing. What had seemed to be an enemy when looking through the eyes of hate or anger, may now be perceived as a troubled soul who needs your compassion.

When we were told that God gave man FREE WILL, we most often believe that what was meant by FREE WILL, was that we could choose one direction or another. We could choose to look both ways before crossing the street, or we could choose to run across without looking. We could choose to take this job, or a different job. We could choose to mow the lawn, or to watch television. We could choose to be kind to others, or we could choose to be disrespectful. We could choose to live a productive life, or we could choose to waste that life.

How many people were aware of the deeper meaning of FREE WILL? How many understood that we are free to see the world in our own unique way? In fact, no one has ever, or will ever, see the world the same way that we each see it. We are free to see someone as our enemy or as Jesus in disguise. We are free to see the Earth as a living entity, and feel great gratitude for it, or to see it as a mass of matter that is there for us to exploit. We are free to see every creature as a creation of God, or just a product of the evolution of matter. We are free to TUNE INTO any bit or type of information that is around us. The amount of information available to us is quite literally infinite, and we will each have our own unique way of filtering whatever information we choose to focus on. The real question is What will we choose to do with this FREEDOM? Will we choose to see life and the world as dangerous and chaotic, or will we choose to see the world as wondrous and magical? We will always be able to find evidence that will "back-up" our views, so why not choose views that make life richer, and full of joy?

What is everything made of? We can choose to believe that everything is made of Matter (something that we have never been able to find,) or we could choose to believe that everything is made of Energy (as though we know what energy is,) or we could choose to believe that consciousness is all that exists.

Story #19-Soul Song

This morning as I sat alone on my couch, I listened to the South Korean singer, Soyang that I have enjoyed hearing so many times. Her voice is angelic and beautiful. When her song was over, I turned off the TV, and prepared myself for a meditation. As I was getting ready, her voice was somehow still singing inside of me, and I began to think about how so many people while describing their "Near Death Experience," have spoken about the most amazing music that they had ever experienced, while on the other side of the veil. When I say they experienced the music, I mean to say that it was much more than just hearing it. Most of them spoke about how the music was alive and penetrated right through them, almost as though they were one with the music. Again, when I say music, that word seems to be the closest as to what our language can describe. In this physical world we experience music through our sense of hearing. Vibrations are picked up and deciphered into what we call sound. In the case of music, the vibrations are created by instruments including the human vocal instrument. Those vibrations travel over some distance, time and space before entering our ears and being deciphered into music.

As I was preparing for my meditation I was suddenly hit with the understanding that what these people had experienced during their NDEs was not music like we have here on Earth, but they were experiencing the actual frequencies of souls! "Hearing" this music was another way of perceiving the multi-dimensionality of souls. Each soul has its own frequency or song that is ever changing, and yet unique to that soul. On the other side of the veil, there are no boundaries. There is no place that a soul ends and another begins, no edges that define it. So to experience the music of a soul does not require time and space, nor does it require ears or some type of deciphering mechanism. Since there are no boundaries for souls, each soul song is experienced directly and instantaneously as though they were part of the perceiving soul.

As this vision or understanding was shown to me, my thoughts went to my deceased wife, and I wondered if it would be possible for me to perceive her soul song during a meditation. There was an excitement building as I pondered if such a thing would be possible. As I finally sat in meditation I found that my guide, "higher self" was ready and already aware of what I wanted to know. Part of me had hoped that my guide would wave his magic wand and I would suddenly be experiencing my wife's song, but I somehow knew that it was not going to be that simple. My guide shared with me that in this physical world we perceive things through our five senses that are all processed through the brain. My brain would not be capable of deciphering the experience of a soul song. He also shared with me that it could still be possible for me to experience her song, but that it would require surrendering my physical awareness. I would have to raise my vibration to a point of forgetting that I even had a body. The thought of being able to experience my wonderful wife in this new way was very exciting. I also found it quite exciting thinking about being able to experience anybody's song in this way. They would not have to be deceased, they could be a loved one, a friend or anyone.

One of my favorite people to listen to has been Ram Dass. I would listen to one of his lectures on YouTube nearly every day and often go to bed with one his lectures on. In one of his talks he spoke about "Somebody Training."[iv] He described how his parents had been "Somebodies" and that as a child his parents set about making him a "Somebody" too. He was made aware of how important it was to be "Somebody" and that the more of a "Somebody" you were, the better off you would be. He spent decades in "Somebody" training and became a real "Somebody." Other people that were great "Somebodies" verified that he was indeed really "Somebody" and that he should be quite proud. Ram shared that even though he was seen as a real "Somebody," he was not happy, his life was not joyful, and he knew that there had to be more to life than just being "Somebody."

I knew that like everyone else, I had gone through extensive "Somebody" training. My parents each had an idea of the "Somebody" that I needed to be, and their visions for what that "Somebody" looked like were quite different. In fact throughout my life, every teacher, family member and friend had a different idea of the "Somebody" that I should be. With all of the training that we go through in life there is little room for our own unique "Soul Song" to be expressed.

As I pondered the suppression of our true soul vibrations, I wondered how much disease is developed from the blocking of this energy. In a real way it seems that all diseases would be able to take hold and grow in an environment where the natural flow of energy is suppressed. As we suppress these energies we create tension, and areas of our bodies contract from that tension. My guide explained how it would be like closing your hand into a fist and then continuing to hold that fist minute after minute, hour after hour, and day after day. If you were able to finally open that hand, you would experience such pain as the blood and energy flowed back in, but most likely areas of the hand would have become permanently damaged after a relatively short time. He explained that when we are under stress, we contract areas of our bodies without even recognizing it, and that these contractions interfere with the natural flow of energy. These areas can begin to lose the ability to function properly, and this can lead to disease. At the very least, suppressing this natural flow of energy would weaken the immune system, dampen the human spirit and make life more challenging.

I'm sure that just about everybody that helped me with my "Somebody" training throughout my life, had my best interest in mind. Each of them most likely believed that they were helping me become a better, more "Normal" person, someone that would fit into this world of "Somebodies." How often have we heard children or even adults say that they just wanted to make their parents proud? Proud of the "Somebody" that they had become. I know that looking back on my life that much of my training was of benefit. Both of my parents had instilled in me that I could accomplish anything that I set my mind to. They really believed that I was capable of great things, but along with that confidence came the other end of the accomplishment stick. If I was not successful it then meant that I must not have done my best, and therefore I had let them down and myself down. I lived my entire life in fear of letting people down. As a General Contractor it was my job to be a problem solver and I had taken this responsibility very seriously. People were relying on me to fix everything. This responsibility and the fear that came with it caused tension in my body, mainly in my shoulders "The weight of the world" and this would cause me to experience frequent headaches.

During my "Somebody" training I learned the "Right Way" of doing many things, like the right way to drive, the right way to show anger or disappointment or love. I was taught how to share, what to share, and what not to share. I was taught that there was no God and no particular reason for life. We live, we die and that's it, if you believe in God it's because you are afraid. I learned that we should respect others unless they prove that they don't deserve that respect.

So today as I write these words, I realize that I don't even know my own "Soul Song." It has been covered up with "Somebody" vibrations that were never my own. I long to experience my wife's "Soul Song," but who would be experiencing her song, the true me or just the "Somebody" that was created through this life that I call mine? So my guide's words, that I would need to raise my vibration to a point of forgetting my physical body, was really saying that I would have to cleanse myself of the "Somebody" vibrations that would never allow me to experience anyone's "Soul Song," even my own. I do believe that I have reached such a vibration during my experiences in Ayahuasca ceremonies, and possibly in several of my past meditations. My meditation this morning was beautiful and a step in the right direction, but I could feel that I was still holding on to so many thoughts. I do plan on doing my future meditations with the main goal of experiencing my own song. Just to have the vision of, and acknowledgement of "Somebody" training, has given me an excitement about a new direction in my meditations.

In my next several meditations I was able to go quite deep and even get to the point of forgetting my physical body. Unfortunately, each time I was brought back to physical awareness because while sitting in the Lotus position, my torso had slumped forward causing enough discomfort to bring me back to my body. I tried a couple of meditations lying down and that didn't quite work out for me. I found it difficult to maintain awareness and kept drifting off into daydreams. I went back to the Lotus position again, asking my guide to help me keep a better posture as I became less aware of my body. This time I was able to go deep enough and found myself back in an experience that I had during an Ayahuasca ceremony.

In almost every Ayahuasca journey I experienced a life where I had been a Native American. I was a large but well built man, and I was with a group of men sitting around a large campfire. I knew that I was held in a position of great respect, not a chief or a medicine man, but somehow a beloved leader. We were in the middle of a ceremony that included the use of Ayahuasca or some other plant medicine. We were all quiet, but I could feel real joy and friendship flowing through and around all of us as though the medicine was connecting us to the one great family. I became aware that all of the other men, even while deep into the medicine journey were somehow waiting for me to laugh. I was still aware enough that I was in my own Ayahuasca ceremony in California, and that the room was filled with people experiencing their own journeys. I did not want to start laughing and interrupt all those around me, but not only was my Native American self expected to laugh, I was somehow being told that I also needed to laugh here and now. I understood that I was to laugh like I had never laughed before. I needed to laugh and let the laughter cleanse my body and soul.

I could hear and feel myself as the Native American begin to laugh. It started as almost a low chuckle and then began to grow in intensity. As he began laughing I began laughing. My laughter grew from the same low chuckle to a full out laugh, and as it gained intensity there were periods where it would switch from a very low pitch into a very high almost young girl laughter. I could hear one by one the people in my ceremony begin laughing. Soon everyone had joined in and the room was filled with a laughter that I had never heard before. Even as I was laughing I could hear my inner voice telling me to keep laughing and let it all out. After several minutes I could feel the laughter begin to subside. There was not an abrupt end, but rather a slow fade followed by brief periods of chuckles and sometimes bursts of laughing. It was such a joy to hear and experience the energy transformation that had taken place in the room. I had been aware of some people crying, and I could feel how they were struggling through the ceremony. The laughter had totally changed their experience and raised the vibration of the entire room. Later the Shaman that had led the ceremony came to where I was sitting and sat next to me and thanked me for the laughter.

The experience had made me realize that throughout my life although I had always loved laughing, whenever I was actually laughing I had always tried to stop laughing. I had never experienced just letting the laughter take me and have me until it was done with me. For the first time in my life I had let the laughter raise my vibration into an experience of myself that I had never known. It felt as though the laughter had moved into every cell of my body and shaken them to the point of releasing long held tensions. My body seemed to be buzzing with energy and clarity.

Later in the ceremony, while still deep into the work of the medicine, I was shown or had the experience of seeing the perfect vibration. It appeared as a stream of energy so intense that it became the purest of light. The light was so pure that nothing could disturb it. I could see what I could only describe as particles of light leaving the stream and other particles rejoining the stream. The particles that were emerging from the stream would immediately change from the perfect white light of the stream into very beautiful particles of white light with hints or glimmers of other colors mixed in. I could feel the vibrations or frequencies of some these light particles leaving the stream, and they carried the same joy that I had experienced while in the middle of my laughter. I understood that these were souls and that they were leaving the stream and were going off to new adventures.

I believe that the absolute joy that we can experience during uncontrolled laughter is most likely the closest to the pure light of creation that we can attain while still in a physical body. They say that laughter is the best medicine, and this would certainly explain why that would be so. The souls leaving the stream and taking on unique colors may be a way of perceiving individual "Soul Songs." Perhaps those colors are the result of adding our own "Point of View" or vibration to how we each perceive reality.

Story #20-Readings

My Mother

The first time that I remember truly tuning into another person was with my mother. She had suffered from migraine headaches since she was fourteen years old. As an adult, it seemed that she had migraines more often than not. She would spend days in her room with the shades closed and a cold washcloth on her head. I had been listening to a lecture from an interesting healer. She described a technique she referred to as "brain balancing." I immediately thought of my mother and was excited to try it out on her.

One day while my mother was in the middle of one of her migraines, I knocked on her bedroom door, and asked if she could come out of her room. She opened the door, still holding the cold washcloth to her head. I explained just a little about what this healer had said, and asked if she would join me in the living room, where I could give it a try. I had a chair from the dining room waiting for her, and she made her way to it and slowly sat down.

I positioned myself behind her and put my hands on her head as the healer had instructed. I began running the energy the way she had described. I was surprised at how easy it was to visualize the flow and sense the current. I could feel the area of my mother's head where the energy seemed to be blocked. I just kept visualizing the flow, loosening and breaking through her blockage. After several minutes of working with the energy, I began to notice a sense of fear coming over me. I didn't understand where the fear was coming from, there didn't seem to be anything for me to be afraid of. As the fear continued to grow, I mentioned it to my mother, saying that I didn't know what I was afraid of. She responded by telling me that she was feeling a great deal of fear. She was afraid that I was doing something to her brain, somehow altering her in a way that frightened her. It was her fear that I was feeling, yet it felt as real to me as if it were my own.

I finished the session, and my mother's headache was completely gone! She sat there trying to find some trace of it, but it had disappeared. She never asked me to use this technique on her again. She had found it unnerving to have me feel her feelings. I'm not sure if she was protecting me from her own fears, or if she just wanted to keep her feelings private. Still, this had been a life altering experience for me. With it came questions and a need for some answers.

Dimensional Healing

As mentioned in a previous story, Dimensional Healing was a class that I took in 2001. The purpose of the class was to learn a specific, hands on technique for helping people with cancer. While I was learning this technique I literally had my hands on people approximately ten hours a day. It was during this class that I became aware of my ability to "read" or tune in to people when I touched them. If I put my hands on someone's shoulder, I would pick up information on what emotions they were holding in that area. If I put my hands over their kidneys, I would pick up what emotions they were holding in that organ.

One day as class had ended, some of us taking the class, and some of the people that were assisting with the class, decided to take turns working on each other. All of these people already had their own healing practices and were there to learn Dimensional Healing to add to their skill sets. I was more interested in this ability that I was discovering, of reading people. One lady was lying on a massage table and getting a treatment from one of the students. I asked her if she would be interested in a reading, which she very eagerly agreed to.

I pulled up a chair and put my right hand on her. Almost immediately, I was overcome with the most beautiful, calm energy that I had ever felt. Even now, nineteen years later, I have never felt someone with such an amazing energy! I just wanted to sit there and be bathed in the comfort and warmth of this wonderful woman. I wondered what type of life she must have lived to be so clear of heavy emotional energies. As I sat there with my hand on her, the word "smooth" kept running through my mind. There were no spikes of energy, just smooth, calm peacefulness.

One of the things I had learned during class time was that as I would pick up information that was being stored in the body, I could ask for a "deeper" level. Sometimes things are stored on what feels like a surface level, but as I would ask or tell myself to go to a deeper level, I would pick up what I would describe as a foundational issue. Something that is so ingrained in the body, that it almost seemed to be part of the body rather than something stored in it.

With my right hand on this sweet lady and feeling so much comfort in her energy, I instructed myself to go to a deeper level. For the first time, I was pulled out of her body and into the energy field that surrounded her. Hidden in this field, I felt a trauma that ran deeper than anything I had experienced during any of my readings. I could feel that the trauma had happened when she was just a child. As I began to tell her what I was seeing/feeling, the information just seemed to flow faster than I could relay it to her. I told her that she had done an amazing amount of work on herself to try and heal this deep wound. I saw that for now, it was not affecting her body, mostly because she had been able to push it out of the body and into this energy field. I could clearly see that this hurt was going to come crashing back into her body in this lifetime, and it would cause such turmoil that it would literally be difficult to survive. Although, over the years she had done so much healing work on herself, this wound had not been healed. From her perspective, the level of forgiveness needed to let this go, did not seem possible.

Years after this reading, the trauma had come back into her life, and although she worked with such strength and purpose to heal it, a deep rage kept rearing its ugly head. After a three year battle with an illness that spread through her body, causing more pain than a person should ever have to endure, she left this planet. She had been one of the most amazing healers that I have ever met. It seems that so many people become healers because they are working on healing themselves, and are driven to help others as they learn to heal their own bodies.

The Hidden Self

One day, while I was attending an Ayahuasca ceremony, I looked across the room and saw a young man sitting and noticed he was moving his legs back and forth looking very nervous. I watched for several minutes, and his legs never stopped this nervous motion. The ceremony had not started yet, and I knew I had time to go chat with him. I sat down next to him and introduced myself. He seemed pleasant but quite nervous. I asked him what was going on that would cause this leg motion. He said that he had been diagnosed with fibromyalgia. I had known a number of people with this diagnosis, but none of them moved with such nervous energy. I asked what he had been told about what the cause of the fibromyalgia might be. He said the doctors had only told him that it was a chemical imbalance. I then asked if it would be okay for me to take a look. He had no idea what I meant, but said sure, go ahead. I placed my right hand on his leg and immediately felt myself tumbling backwards through space.

In doing my readings, sometimes words come to me, sometimes sounds or visions, and sometimes I feel what the person I am touching feels. There are times that I need to interpret what I see and feel, almost like interpreting a dream. This time, I began talking before I even had a chance to interpret what was happening. It felt as though the information just flowed out of me. I said, "In your entire life, you have never felt that you had a safe place to land or to stand. Your parents loved you, but you felt that you had to be who they needed you to be, in order to receive that love. In your entire life you never had a friend that you felt safe for you to be you around. You have spent your life trying to be who everyone else needed you to be, never feeling safe to let yourself just be you. You are ever vigilant, looking around and trying to figure out who you need to be in each moment, living in fear that if you let yourself be you, no one would accept you. It is this constant fear that is the root cause of the fibromyalgia."

I had never met this young man before and knew nothing about him, yet as the words flowed out of me, I had no doubt of their accuracy. When I had finished, he looked at me with a look of gratitude, like I was the first person that truly understood him. His secret was out and perhaps he need not pretend any more. He said, "That is exactly my life. I know my parents loved me, but I couldn't really be me around them." I gave him a hug and went back to my spot on the other side of the room. I wondered if hearing this information would help him or not.

Jasmine

It was mid-June, a beautiful sunny day at my home in the mountains of California. I received a phone call from one of my guests in an Airbnb that I have on my property. It was being rented by a couple of very young ladies that were sisters. I was told that Jasmine, the older of the two, had fallen and hit her head on the tile floor. They were wanting to know where the closest hospital was. I quickly checked and found that there was an urgent care facility open just a few miles away. I gave them the information and directions and off they went.

They had only arrived at my place a day earlier, and they had really made an impact on me. As I was showing them the property, Jasmine had asked if it was just me and my wife that lived here. I immediately felt a tear form and make its way down my cheek. My wife had passed only a month earlier, and my life was turned upside down. I told them about her passing and they both shed a tear. I told them that Second Hand Lions was one of her favorite movies, and that Jasmine was the name of two of the important characters in the movie, a fact that didn't escape my notice when Jasmine and her sister had first booked my guest place. We then walked over to look at the hot tub and Jasmine perked up a little and said, "Tomorrow's my birthday, and we came here to celebrate." I looked at her in disbelief! It was also my wife's birthday! This time, I held back my tears; I didn't want to take anything away from her celebration. When I finished going over all the things they needed to know about the place, I went back into my house and wondered if my wife was somehow responsible for these two young ladies being here. Had she guided them from the other side?

While they were in urgent care, I was quite concerned about Jasmine's condition. I pondered over what had happened to her, falling backward in a chair and hitting her head. From my experience with "accidents," I believed there is no such thing. For me, there had to be a reason that she hit, and hurt her head rather than hurting some other part of her body. Also, this happened here on my property, bringing it into a shared experience.

They were gone a couple of hours and upon returning, went right into the cottage, where I didn't hear a peep out of ether of them all evening. The next morning, I sent Jasmine a text, asking how she was doing. She responded that the doctor had told her she most likely had a concussion. She was still not feeling very well. I asked if she would be alright with me coming over to the cottage and visiting with her and her sister. Jasmine texted back, that I was welcome to stop in.

They both greeted me at the door and invited me in. They were both so sweet and I think they were worried that I might be upset at them for the "horsing around" that had caused the accident. We all sat down, and I explained that I did not believe in accidents, and that I felt that all this had happened for a reason. I told them a little about how I would read people and I asked if it would be alright for me to read Jasmine. I don't think that they had ever heard of such a thing before, but Jasmine agreed to let me give her a reading. She was sitting in the very chair that she had fallen over in. I got up and stood behind her and put my right hand on her right shoulder.

I could feel myself falling backwards just as she had done. I understood that in this case the falling backward was a reference to not moving forward in the direction that she wanted to. As I was experiencing the information that was coming to me, I started relaying it to her the best that I could. I told her that there was something in her life that she had a passion for, most likely a direction that she wanted to go with her life. I could see that her parents were not particularly happy with this direction and were pressuring her to live her life the way they saw best. Hitting her head on the floor was her way of protesting, and calling attention to her own desires. It reminded me of the phrase, "getting hit upside the head to get your attention."

Almost as soon as I started describing what I was seeing and feeling, Jasmine had begun to cry. By the time I was finished with the reading, she was sitting there sobbing, tears running down her cheeks and dropping from her chin. I moved back to my chair and let her have some time to move into a calmer place. I looked over at her sister, who was sitting on the edge of the bed and also in tears. She knew Jasmine's story and was moved to share her grief. After a couple of minutes, Jasmine looked over at me and said that what I had described was exactly what was happening in her life. Jasmine said that they had actually come to my place to get away from the pressure she was feeling from her parents, and to ponder what she might do with her life.

These two young ladies had come to my home and touched my life in profound ways. I have no doubt that it had all been orchestrated by my wife, who I knew was still looking out for me from wherever she was. When they left, they each hugged me as though we had always been family.

Could I take a peek

While taking a class, learning Bowen Therapy, I met a man from Iran. I think there were around sixteen people taking the class and we would pair up to practice different techniques on each other. I often chose this man to partner with because he always seemed to be so happy. He was a pleasure to talk with and to be around. I remember him telling me how he and his wife would wake up every day and turn on some lively music. First thing in the morning, they would be listening to this music and dancing as they went about getting ready for work and making breakfast. Each time they would run into each other, they would dance together for a minute, and then go about whatever they had to do.

He was one of the few genuinely happy people that I have ever known. He had made it a point to start every day happy and to carry that joy throughout the day. As we were learning new Bowen moves, I would be practicing on him and could feel the joy that he carried in his body. It felt light and open and refreshing. I know that he enjoyed my company too. I think he was as happy to partner with me, as I was to work with him.

One day, he was a little late getting to class, and as he walked in, I could see that he was not the joyful man that I had become accustomed to. Through most of the class that day, there was instruction with very little partner practice going on. When finally we were pairing up to practice, he went right over to a lady and partnered with her. It was not unusual for us to partner with other people, and it gave me the chance to work with a young lady that I had not partnered with before. As with just about everyone that was involved in learning healing techniques, this young lady was so sweet and happy to help others. I really enjoyed working with her, but I kept wondering what was up with my friend.

As we were getting close to the end of the class for the day, I finally had a chance to greet him, and I asked what was troubling him. He looked at me with such sad eyes, and just said that he didn't want to talk about it. This was not like him at all, and I was not ready to just let him be. I didn't want him to be so unhappy. I said, "If you don't want to tell me, could I take a peek?" I knew that he had no idea what I was talking about, but he asked what I meant by take a peek.

I put my right hand on his heart and opened the space for information to come. I was hit with such sadness but could not see what was causing it. With my hand still on his heart, I would ask a question out loud, not for him, but a question for myself. I asked if the sadness had to do with work and received the knowing that it was not about his work. I asked if the sadness had to do with his wife and immediately knew that it was not about her. I didn't know anything about his family, but I asked if the sadness had to do with his family. I felt a solid yes; this was where the sadness was coming from. I asked if it had to do with a daughter and again a solid yes.

My friend is just standing there, listening to me ask questions, and answering myself. He was not giving me any clues as to my accuracy, but he was obviously very intrigued by what I was doing. I began asking myself questions about his daughter, that I did not even know he had. I asked if she had been in an accident and knew that she had not. I asked if it had to do with her school or work, and again understood that it was not either of those. I asked if someone had hurt her feelings and immediately received a yes. As I focused on this information, I could see/feel people ridiculing her, bullying her because of the color of her skin and belittling her because she was from Iran. I could feel that she had been full of the same joy that her parents would start every day with. She was full of life and so happy to be alive and have friends. Then with this experience, it was like a wave of heaviness had washed over her, washing away the joy of life and making her feel shame for where she had been born and for how others viewed her.

That same heaviness had also washed over both of her parents. I could feel tears welling up inside me as I felt her pain and now her father's pain. He loved his daughter with such unconditional love and so much pride. Now here was this thing that he could not protect her from. His sadness ran to the core of his being. As I shared all of this with him, he could not speak. I looked at him and hugged him, telling him how sorry I was for his grief and that of his family. We never did talk about it again. The class went on for several more weeks, but my friend had not been able to get back to the happy man that he had been.

The young people that had bullied his daughter could have no idea of the ripples that they had unleashed on the world. They had only been words, but they had been filled with emotional content. My friend's daughter would most likely carry those words with her for the rest of her life. My friend and his wife would also never forget her torment. I was a very minor player in their lives, and yet I was touched and changed by words uttered by people that I would never meet. Those words, said out of anger or fear, rippled through me, and now as I share them here, they ripple to you. This is how life works, and perhaps when enough people have been sufficiently rippled with ignorant, hurtful words, they won't be needed any longer.

Bianca

My phone beeped, indicating a message from Airbnb. When I had time to take a look at it, there was a new booking for a lady named Bianca. The cottage that I rent is a single room with a bathroom and a small kitchenette. Almost all of my bookings have been couples, sometimes two ladies and a few times a couple of young men. This time the booking indicated that it was for just one person. I believe that this was only the second time that a single person had booked the room. I wondered if it was a mistake and would not be surprised to see two people pull into the driveway. I have an alarm at the top of the driveway, so I would know when a guest would be arriving.

Even though the country was in the middle of the Covid 19 pandemic, my cottage had been quite busy, with almost constant bookings. In years past, my guests have been from all over the world. It was such a pleasure to meet and chat with people that were here touring America. My place is just twenty-five minutes from the gate into Yosemite National Park, so most of my guests were here to visit this amazing wonder. This year, with the virus, just about every one of my guests had been from California, people just needing to get away, and feel that they were not in lock down.

Days before Bianca was to arrive, I started having feelings like this was going to be a special experience. I was already wondering if my recently passed wife was once again spinning her loving magic and influencing the course of my life. Every day, I could feel her presence, like a warm blanket comforting me, and helping to cope with the almost unbearable sense of loss that I had felt since she had left me here to finish life without having her hand to hold.

When Bianca pulled into the driveway, I could see that she was indeed by herself. As I would with all of my guests, I met her as she was parking the car. With my Covid 19 mask on, I gave her a tour of the room, and the area around the cottage. She was a beautiful young black woman, with a wonderful smile, and had a very pleasant energy about her. She said that she was just looking to get away for a few days, and this was a kind of working vacation. She explained that much of her work was on the phone, so she was able to work from almost anywhere.

My wife had set up our ad on the Airbnb website, which included pictures of the cottage, descriptions of some of the surroundings, and her own profile with a picture of herself. I have not had the heart to change our ad since her passing. Even as I write this some eight months later, it is still her profile, and picture on the website. In it, she mentions that she is a body worker, and as fate would have it, Bianca tells me that she has been in some pain and was hoping that my wife could work on her.

After telling Bianca of my wife's passing, I shared that I have been trained in Bowen therapy, and would be happy to work on her myself. We set up a time for the session, and we both went about our day. Bowen therapy is a light touch type of body work where several "moves" are performed and then the client is left for several minutes to let their body adjust to the work. My wife had been trained in this type of therapy and when she started practicing it on me, I was surprised to see that it was making real changes, that were actually getting rid of problems that I had dealt with for years. Upon noticing how well I was doing from her work on me, my wife told me that I had to take Bowen classes myself, so that I could work on her. I happily agreed and loved learning this wonderful healing technique. It was absolutely worth the months of training.

Bianca arrived right on time for our appointment, and I had a massage table set up and waiting for her. She explained that her pain was in many different areas of her body, and that she did not know what was causing this amount of discomfort. After she made herself comfortable on the table, I performed a few "moves" to relax her body and began to talk with her about the readings that was able to do. I explained how we carry beliefs and emotions in different areas of our bodies. I asked if she would be interested in a "general" reading. This is a reading where I don't need to have my hand on a specific area, and am just looking for the general state or condition of the body. She readily agreed.

After performing several more Bowen moves, I pulled up an office chair, and gently placed my right hand on her. Almost right away I began to feel a great deal of turmoil. There was so much information coming through that it was difficult to decipher. The information was in the form of images and emotions. At times, I would see images of small groups of black people looking up through a small square door. I believe that I was looking down through this door into a hold on a ship or boat. The emotions seemed to be as though these people were terrified, wanting out of the hold, and yet afraid of what might await them on the outside. I felt the agony of families being torn apart by force, and what seemed to be unimaginable suffering. It was as if Bianca was holding the suffering of the entire African American race in her little body, and now with my hand on her, I was experiencing it too! It had never occurred to me, that the history of a race could be carried in a body. I wondered if it was being held in cellular memory or in some way that I was unfamiliar with.

I pulled my hand away, and performed a couple more Bowen moves on her. I shared one of the images that I had seen with her and told her that she was holding some intense emotions concerning her race. I didn't feel that it would be beneficial for me to tell her of the depth of the turmoil that I had felt, but I did share that if she did not release some of this energy, it could manifest as a serious problem in her body. In fact, it was most likely this stored energy/information that was causing the physical pains that she was experiencing. I finished the Bowen session, and Bianca went back to the cottage for the evening.

This relatively short reading had opened my mind to possibilities that I had not thought of before. If Bianca could somehow be holding the history of a race in her body, could a woman hold the history of women? Could a man hold the history of men? When we are born into this earthly plain, do we don a body suit that comes with information based on race, origin or sex? Even as I asked these questions silently in my own mind, I felt they were being answered. I was told/shown that information exists in the infinite field of awareness. This includes all of human history. We can access the history of a race, a gender, a country, a religion or any type of group consciousness. I don't mean to imply that this information is always negative, on the contrary, we might access information on Jesus or Buddha. We might access information on compassion or love, or on health or science or art or music. This would explain child prodigies that can write or play music at very early ages. It could explain how artists can create such masterful works.

It seems that because of the great amount of persecution and suffering that so many black people have endured, it is quite common for them to access the historical race information. Once this history has been accessed, it is turned on in the body and may be responsible for many of the illnesses that are more prevalent among their race. Along with the information, there is also an emotional content that can bring feelings of anger, fear, rage, shame and unworthiness. Each emotion can bring chaos and conflict that the human body does not know how to cope with, and may manifest in numerous ways.

Women throughout history, have often been treated as second class, or less than their male counterpart. Even in the history of the United States, women have rarely been treated as equals, whether in voting rights, business positions or in wages. Bianca had shared with me, that she believed black women are the most hated group in America! Could it be that black women could carry not only the anguish of the black race, but also the suppression of women?

As I pondered the role of women in the world and especially black women, I am humbled by their amazing strength; so many have been left to raise children on their own as a single parent. Somehow, women find a way to make it work. Women seem to be generally more able or willing to feel vulnerable, and allow their hearts to be more open. They feel compassion for others at a level that is less evident among men.

I would like to say that as a man I am aware of my tuning into the group consciousness of men. If it hadn't been for my reading with Bianca, I would not have understood or viewed my role as a man in this new way. Now I see that my view of what a man is supposed to be, has been formed by more than just the teachings of my parents. By watching movies that included westerns, war, love stories or action thrillers; I see that I "tuned into" the emotions of the characters, the beliefs of the characters, and could understand how each of those men viewed their role as a man. The same is true for reading books or even just chatting with other men. There is a history of manhood that is somehow stored in the recesses of consciousness. My understanding of what a man is supposed to be, was slowly created through out my life. "Tuning into" the group consciousness of men meant tuning into the emotions, the fears, the traumas, and the duties of men. It also meant tuning into the accomplishments, the successes, and the victories. All aspects of the history of men are stored in the group consciousness. Many consider this to be a "Mans World," a world that may seem easier or more supportive for men. I can say that from my own experience of being a man, that my life has been filled with fear. I have often felt the fear of not living up to what my view of a being a man meant. Could I always be the provider, the protector, the problem solver? After watching so many war movies with my father, and hearing of his experiences in WW2, it was easy to tune into the suffering of so many young men. The horrors of war have plagued the planet for thousands of years, so the amount of suffering and trauma in the group consciousness is immense. There are also the beliefs that if we are fired from a job, have a lover leave us, or endure some financial loss, we have failed as a man.

No matter which "Group" we see ourselves belonging to, there is a history of that group that exists in the field of consciousness. So many groups, such as; men, women, Christian, Jewish, Muslim, Black, Native American, Aboriginal, war veterans, Communist, Socialist, Democrat, Republican, American, Chinese, African, gay, straight, athlete, overweight, handicapped, alcoholic, poor, wealthy, single, married, mother, father, intellectual, emotional, each having their own sets of beliefs, values and ways of perceiving the world. Most of us see ourselves as belonging to more than just one group, and have to find ways of intermingling our beliefs about each group. We can "tune into" the higher vibrational aspects of the groups that we identify with, or we can tune into the lower aspects of each group. We can resonate with the joys, triumphs and blessings of our groups, or we can resonate with the suffering, the traumas and the limitations of those groups.

Which groups we identify with change, our view or perspective of life. Just like every word represents meaning and helps to describe some part of life, so do the groups that we identify with. Just as every word comes with limitations and can never describe the true nature or truth of anything, every group comes with limited views, and most often keep us in a self created box. Truth defies limitations and can never be held by any group. True freedom can only come through the surrender of beliefs and limitations. In my understanding, to identify with any group is to accept the beliefs and limitations of that group.

Story #21-Transformation

Transformation is defined as "A thorough or dramatic change in form or appearance." This morning my meditation was dedicated to understanding, or looking at what transformation looks like from a human, and perhaps even from a soul perspective. There are so many facets or ways of perceiving this thing called transformation. I believe that during the writing of this story, there will be more meditations, more research and dialogs with what I find to be experts in the fields of Quantum Mechanics, Neuroscience and religions.

In my meditation I was shown how, from birth into this physical world, we become "Interpreters." We learn to interpret the pains in our stomach as the signal that we need to eat. We learn that the loving touch of our mother can soothe our fears. We learn to interpret the brightness of light into day, and darkness into night. We learn to interpret the tone of a voice as loving or angry. Throughout life we continue to interpret and give meanings to everything. The quicker we learn to interpret signals into meanings, the safer we are, the more we understand the world.

Our parents are perhaps the most responsible for how we learn to interpret and give meanings to physical reality. We also have teachers in our schools, siblings, friends, relatives, religions, television, books, computers, and our own life experiences that help us interpret life. So in a way we create our personal set of viewing glasses that tell us how to see the world. We become so adept at interpreting, and then being able to recall those interpretations, that often we don't need to interpret a new situation, and instead can simply categorize it as being similar to a past situation, and then apply the old interpretation. As an example, if as a child you were bitten by a dog, and found that event both frightening and painful, years later you may view all dogs as potential threats. You would remember the interpretation from the past, and then apply that same interpretation to this new experience.

EVERY interpretation is a point of view, and does not include the whole story, nor does it mean that the truth of a thing has been uncovered. Instead, we have decided not to look any farther into this object, person or situation, because we have labeled it, categorized it, and filed it into memory to be recalled when we need it again. Through life we continue this same process whether it is how we see our parents, siblings, friends, animals, work, science, health, the stars, the universe or even GOD. Nothing escapes the powers of interpretation. What this means is that we go through life seeing everything through lenses that obscure the fullness and richness of the world. We are literally perceiving only a small fraction of the Human Experience.

As an example, we have probably all known someone that has been addicted to alcohol. For them, the alcohol might be interpreted as a method of escape from their daily life, or it might be interpreted as something that gives them permission to express themselves in a different way. They may see the alcohol as the catalyst to "Transform" into someone other than who they believe themselves to be. For some people drinking wine, beer or even a mixed drink, might be seen as a way to relax or unwind. For some people having a drink with a friend might just be a way of socializing. There are also those that may have a drink just because they really enjoy the flavors. Then there are those that have made a business out of making and selling alcohol. For each of these instances what the alcohol means for the individual is quite different; so we can see that alcohol has indeed been interpreted to be something or mean something different. In the case of the alcoholic, the alcohol was meant to provide "Transformation".

We would normally think of transformation as a positive event, but it can also be a move into a less loving, less kind, and less conscious way of behaving.

For another example of interpretation, let's look at an oak tree. We might view the tree as a loving giant that provides shade for our home. We might view it as a symbol of strength and longevity. We might see it as lumber for some building project. We might see it as a home for birds, insects and all kinds of life. We might see it as a potential threat if it looms over our home. A child might see it as the perfect place to practice their climbing skills. Few people would see the tree in the larger picture that includes all of the above, but also how it harmonizes with the environment. It produces offspring that it actually may nurture. It provides for all types of life below the surface of the soil. It interacts with the air, wind and rain. These views still do not even include looking at the tree through quantum glasses that attempt to look at how the tree came into existence. The quantum world is an entirely different experience where the whole of the tree is hardly noticed, because we are looking at what might seem to be an infinite number of pieces of awareness that come into and then back out of existence. You could spend years studying an oak tree, and still would not understand all there is to know about the tree.

So as we look at an oak tree, we generally see it only through whatever interpretation that we have assigned to it, and never bother to look any farther. It's easy to see how any interpretation of the tree gives only a fraction of the true experience of an oak tree. This is the case for EVERYTHING that we see, hear, feel and believe. If we only know one percent of the experience of a tree, then perhaps that is close to what we actually know about anything. Yet we have interpreted and given meaning to just about everything that we have encountered in life. We believe that we have interpreted everything correctly, and will often argue fervently to protect our "Rightness" of our interpretation.

Humans have inhabited the Earth for thousands of years. It has provided a place to stand, to build a home on and the materials to build that home. It provides food and water. It has protected us from the Sun's radiation and yet lets the sun's light shine upon it. The Earth has allowed for the survival of millions and perhaps hundreds of millions of species of life, providing for each life form just what it has needed to develop and live. There seems to be a system that regulates temperature, moisture and the delicate balance of breathable air. At this point in history, the amount of information that is accessible regarding our planet is amazing. Anyone with access to a computer or even a cell phone can get more information about the planet than they can even absorb. Even with all this information at our fingertips, all seven billion of us still interpret the Earth in our own unique way. For many, the planet and all of its resources are something to exploit and profit from. For some the planet is something to explore and enjoy. For some, the Earth is seen as sacred, and they believe that humans are its caretakers. There are those that believe the Earth is actually a living, conscious life form of its own. Many only see the Earth as the place that we live, and there is enough to worry about just trying to get through daily life, that concern for the well-being of the planet is too much to ask. There are many that have made the study of the Earth or its inhabitants their passion and their business.

Again, it is easy to see that there are infinite ways of seeing, understanding and interpreting the Earth. Each interpretation is one hundred percent right, but also one hundred percent limited. This is the case for every interpretation about everything. We could go on looking at Love, marriage, children, schooling, religion, business, friendships, technology and anything else that you want, but we will always be able to interpret whatever we are looking at in our own unique way.

So why is this thing called interpretation so important? Why does it matter that we each interpret everything in life in our own unique way? Because we are discussing the topic of Transformation, and how we interpret life has everything to do with Transformation. To accomplish a thorough and dramatic change means that we have to be different than how we were in the past. Others would have to be able to look at us and see that we are somehow different than how they have known us to be. We must feel different internally, and that means that we have to have made a great change.

For some, Transformation occurs when they accept God or Jesus into their lives. For some Transformation can happen when they have a child, and suddenly understand that they must be more than they had allowed themselves to ever be before, for the sake of this new little life. For some Transformation can take place when they find a job or career that they have a real passion for. This job is literally a new beginning for them, and they may blossom into an entirely different person. For some Transformation may take place after some traumatic event that alters how they now interpret life.

In each case Transformation takes place when life is seen from a new perspective. Transformation is literally a change in interpretation, and can only take place when some part of life is seen from a new point of view. As our point of view is changed, so our life is changed. As an example, we have all seen on the news a mother pouring out grief at the death of her child, expressing hate and vengeance towards that child's killer. The loss of that child may have Transformed this mother into a hollow shell of her former self. Life for her has become one of anguish and sorrow. We have also witnessed a grieving mother express forgiveness towards the killer, and although this act does not bring the child back, nor does it ease the grieving, it does allow her to have a much brighter interpretation for life. Her act of forgiveness also brings about the Transformation of her life. The loss of the child also may bring about an expanded awareness of the depth of the Love that the mother truly felt for her child. Before the loss took place, "Normal" life was happening, which probably included many differing points of view between the mother and child, and most likely included upsets, disappointments and even some anger with each other. Then after the loss, a much larger view of the relationship may be experienced, including the understanding of how insignificant those differing points of view truly were. The loss may actually allow for the Mother to experience a deeper, more unconditional love than she had ever felt before: her expanded understanding of Love literally Transforming her view of life, and the connections with those around her.

As I am writing this part of the story, it has been more than a year and half since my wife made her transition from this physical world. To say that I have missed her every day would not do the feelings justice. There are still times that the depth of loss seems almost unbearable, yet there are more and more days that I find myself just feeling such gratitude that she chose to spend so much of her life with me. During our many years together, I had always thought that I was doing a wonderful job of expressing my admiration and love for her, but through the past year, I have come to view love from a much larger perspective. I can now see that my expressions of admiration and love were but a shadow of what she actually meant to me. Because of her loss, I now have a greater understanding and appreciation for love, and the many ways that we can express that love. It is once again more evidence that from suffering we seem to grow the most. I had always recognized that our relationship had helped me grow emotionally, spiritually, and as a person in general, but now I see that in her death I have grown even more in all of these ways. This growth that I am speaking of is another way of describing Transformation. Growth means that we are understanding something in a new and larger way, we are viewing life from a greater perspective. It also seems that no matter how large of a perspective we are able to gain, as long as we are in this physical world, we are most likely not capable of perceiving anything in its entirety.

Each time we are able to expand our interpretation of a situation, there is a feeling of expansion, a sensation of more space and more freedom. There may also be the recognition of letting go of a subtle contraction that we had been holding. That contraction is literally a squeezing off of energy that we have been holding in some part of our body. The letting go of this contraction, allows for greater energy flow, and that wonderful feeling of expansion and space. We have been Transformed by the release of the old points of view, and are now experiencing the world with greater clarity. When we consider that we have hundreds and perhaps thousands of points of view that are creating contractions throughout our bodies, it's difficult to even imagine what we might be capable of physically, emotionally and spiritually, if we could somehow release the majority of those stifling beliefs. Yet we hold on to them as though our lives depended on them.

If we were to imagine a time when we were sick and needed to stay home for a few days, and that we are sitting on the couch with the TV remote in hand, and we could choose to watch anything that we wanted. We could watch murder mystery after murder mystery, or we could watch one love story after another, or we could watch one adventure movie after another, where the hero would have to overcome one obstacle after another. We could choose to watch horror movie after horror movie or comedy after comedy. Some of us might choose to watch nothing but news or perhaps sports. The point is that whatever we choose is most likely the same type of show that we have always chosen. Whatever we choose, we are trading that amount of our time for that type of experience. In life we often choose to live today the same way that we lived yesterday and the day before that and so on. Life becomes a habit of choosing the same thing over and over again, just like choosing the type of show we are going to watch. Our choices are directly related to our points of view and how we see the world.

Our points of view are just another way of describing our interpretations. Our thoughts are the way that we continue to play points of view and interpretations through our mind. Everything that we experience is filtered through our mind's interpretations. There are three parts to give us our actual experience of each moment. There is something that we are perceiving, such as an object or situation; then there is how our mind filters or interprets what we are perceiving; and then there is how we feel about that object or situation. If any of these three factors are removed, there would not be an experience or at least the awareness of an experience.

If you were to be sitting outside in a beautiful meadow, surrounded by trees and a small creak running next to you, there would be thousands of places to put your attention; the sunlight, the warmth of the sun, a light breeze, the sound of the wind through the trees, the sound of the creek or the movement of the water. You could be aware of the feeling of the grass you're sitting on, or the position of your foot, or the feeling of the shirt you have on. You could be lost in thought and not even be aware of any of these things, and instead be focused on your work or your family. You could be pondering the workings of the universe, and your place in it. Literally there is no limit to what you might choose to place your attention on, and whatever that choice is, brings with it your thoughts and feelings, completing the trilogy of what it takes to create your experience.

Any of the three factors of experience may take place first. You might see a bird and then your mind may begin to filter what a bird means to you, and then you might feel the freedom and joy of that bird soaring through the sky, and now you have that as your experience of the moment. You might then remember a pet bird that you had as a child and suddenly feel or remember the sadness of its loss. This feeling of sadness may then bring up other times that you felt a similar way.

So we can see that your experience can be initiated from a feeling, a thought or a perception, but all three are needed to actually have an experience. Because we have spent our lives interpreting, labeling, and defining everything that enters our perception, we have generally developed patterns of thinking and behaving. Most of us recognize that there are areas of our lives that we wish were different. We might wish that our boss would show more appreciation for our work; we might wish that a loved one was not addicted to drugs or alcohol; we might wish that our government would be more responsive to our perceived needs, or we might wish that we were in better health. We might believe that we just can't be happy until the particular situation improves. Our thoughts go round and round in our minds trying to find a solution, a way to fix the problem. Most of us have more than one issue that we feel needs to change before we allow ourselves to be happy.

If we look again at what it takes to create our experience, there are just the same three factors; what we perceive, what we think about the situation and then how we feel about the situation. Most people believe that what needs to change is the situation, or someone else's behavior, but this is just one of the three points of experience. The other two points being what we think about it, and how we feel about it. We want to change the one point that we have no control over. We want to remain just as we are but have our experience change. We believe that by having the point of perception change, that we will be Transformed into a happier person. The other two points that create our experience are totally within our control, but we have generally become addicted to our ways of interpreting and feeling. From where we are standing, our points of view make total sense, and we are unwilling to change them. Yet it is this very thing that we are unwilling to do, that is our doorway to true transformation. By allowing ourselves to see a situation from a larger perspective, we allow for a greater understanding, and may suddenly feel different about the whole thing.

A perfect example of transformation is the story of Ebenezer Scrooge, in the book "A Christmas Carol." With the help of some wonderful spirits, Ebenezer was able to see life and money from a much larger perspective, and the result was a total Transformation of his life! Not one part of the actual situation needed to change in order for this transformation to occur; instead, what changed, was first how he saw the situation, and as his view of it changed, so did his feelings shift, causing a completely different experience of the same situation. Ebenezer became a different or Transformed person by the allowing of his interpretation of life to change.

By his change in behavior, there is a ripple that goes out from person to person, each having the choice of expanding the ripples of joy, or choosing whatever emotions they may be addicted to.

We have become so addicted to our ways of thinking and feeling, that there doesn't appear to be room for a larger perspective. As another example, let's say that your four year old child comes running up to you frightened about a spider in the house. She pulls you into the bathroom and points up to the corner of the ceiling. There you see a spider beginning to spin a web. How you as an adult see this situation, and how you react to it, will influence your child for the rest of their life. You could show fear of this little creature and find the quickest, safest way of killing and disposing of the spider; or you could be brave and find a container to trap the spider, and then release it outside; or you could point out to your child the truly magical way the spider can create a web. My sister had been in this exact situation and she not only chose for her and her little girl to watch the web be made, but she allowed the spider to live for years in the bathroom, and watching the spider became something that the two of them enjoyed together.

I am not suggesting that we all let every insect take up residence in our home, but there are different ways of reacting to each situation, and how we react has everything to do with our interpretations, and the ripples that we send out into the world. By showing compassion for the smallest of creatures, we are rippling that compassion in ways that we will never know. Understanding that there are so many ways of interpreting every situation is the beginning of allowing for the possibility of transformation. The next step is to understand that how you interpret the situation affects how you feel; and how you feel effects how you see and interact with all of life; and how you interact with life continually sends ripples around the world.

So how can we become the creators of our own Transformation? How much sadness, unhappiness, turmoil and upset are we willing to endure, before we say enough is enough? Do we have to reach bottom before we are willing to reach for a higher reality? How many low vibrational ripples will we send out to the world, before we acknowledge that we have so much more to offer? How would we behave if we truly understood that everything we did rippled through the world?

In writing this story, much in my life has changed. I have been able to look at my own life from many different viewpoints, and there have been times that seeing my behaviors from a larger perspective has caused me to literally laugh out loud. I have always found it difficult to stay calm while driving my vehicle. My father had made a point of pointing out every mistake other drivers would make, even finding special names or adjectives to describe them. Nearly fifty years later, I find that I still have this ability that my father bestowed upon me. I am able to instantly notice when someone is not paying attention to how they are driving, and can see it through my father's filter of rightness. It seems silly that I have allowed myself to become upset hundreds or perhaps even thousands of times, from how I have judged others' abilities at driving. The funniest part is that I have not witnessed anyone making an error driving that I have not at some point made that same error. Still I have kept this rightness filter, and have traded what could have been relaxing wonderful drives, for the experience of being right about the proper way to drive. I have wasted hours of my life being in turmoil, when I could have simply seen these driving errors with humor, or even a type of camaraderie, recognizing that I had committed the same error before.

If I would like to be able to get behind the wheel and enjoy my driving experience, I cannot expect that every driver is going to drive the way that I would like them to. Instead, for my driving experience to be Transformed, I would need to adopt a greater point of view about driving. By changing how I see and feel about driving errors, my total experience of driving can shift from one of turmoil, to one of pleasure. How we perceive and judge everything has everything to do with our experience of the world. We continually believe that we need a person, an object, or the world to change, in order for us to be happy, but Transformation occurs only when we change how we see the world. If the truth of this is really understood, we become empowered, because nothing outside of us can be blamed for how we feel. We no longer need the world to be different in order for us to vibrate at a level of happiness, joy or love. We become Transformed by surrendering old points of view that truly do not serve us. As this Transformation takes place, we change the ripples that we send out into the world, and change the world in ways that we will never know.

We have become great interpreters, able to see just about anything and give meaning to it, thinking that we understand the totality of it. For those that are seeking a greater understanding of life, and intuitively know that life has to be so much more than it seems to be, the journey has to begin by opening our minds to that greater reality. We soon recognize that the interpretations and definitions that we have been taught or succumbed to are but a shadow of the whole story. We must make room for our interpretations to expand. If every interpretation is less than one percent of the truth of a thing, then there should be plenty of room for that interpretation to grow. To be ridgid and unwilling to look farther, keeps us locked or stuck in an extremely limited life.

So Transformation begins by accepting that greater potentials exist, and that our views are the very things that are limiting us. By just having this single understanding, we create the opportunity for new information to be presented, and hopefully even welcomed. The next step is to recognize that our desire for this larger perspective is stronger and greater than the belief in the rightness of the very limited view from the past. We must embrace this new larger perspective and accept it as our new brighter truth. Step three is to be on guard and notice whenever the prior limiting belief tries to creep into our thoughts, and be ready to say "wait a minute, this is not my belief any more." We should be able to feel the difference between the old limiting perspective, and the new expanded view. When we view from the old perspective, we will feel a very real contraction and lowering of our vibration; while with our new expanded view, there is a feeling of expansion and lightness.

The more that we accept that all of our views are limited and never the whole truth, the more willing and able we are to welcome Transformation. Each time that we expand or transform our understandings, we create a pathway through our egoic blockages that make it easier and easier for new information to be accepted and integrated into our life experience. We even begin to expect and welcome these shifts.

As one more example of the limits of our points of view, imagine that I were to hold up a cell phone in such a way that all that can be seen from where you are standing is the thin line of the bottom of the phone. To you it just looks like a small black strip of plastic. For someone standing by my side, they see the entire back of the phone and it looks like a black plastic rectangle. For someone standing to my other side, they would see the screen of the phone and most likely recognize it as a cell phone. If I were to move the screen of the phone right up against their eyes, they would no longer be able to see enough of the phone to know what it is. If I were to move far enough away, again the phone would become unrecognizable. Whatever angle the phone is viewed from is a valid point of view, yet they are all quite limiting. Even for those that have a clear enough view, to recognize the phone as a phone, how many would understand what makes the phone work? How many could explain the interior workings, or even have a general idea of what each part does? Each point of view is a part of the whole, but no matter where you stand, you can never see the entire phone, including all the interior workings of the phone. For the person that can only see the bottom strip of the phone, the plastic strip is their reality, and until they can move to another viewing position, their knowledge of what I hold in my hand is as limited as their view.

How afraid and stuck must we be to believe that our perspective of any person, place, object or situation, is the only way of seeing it, and that we need to argue, and hold on to that very limiting view? If we know that every point of view that we have is limited, and never encompasses the entire truth, then it would seem that the more we truly desire to know and understand anything, the more we are prepared to open our minds and hearts to greater truths. We all have areas in our lives that we wish were different, from our health, our wealth, our relationships or our emotional wellbeing. When we begin to understand that every aspect of our lives is a product of our points of view, we finally grasp that we are in charge of our own happiness and fulfillment. There is the recognition that we don't need the world to change to fit our vision, but instead we must change our vision of the world. This is truly the definition of Transformation, to see the world in a new way.

How do we see the world with new eyes? When our patterns of thoughts and beliefs have become so ingrained, how can we ignore the ways that we see and know the world? As much as we might desire something in the world to change, that very change can only take place by shifting our perspective of it. So many people would rather hold on to their "Rightness" of their points of view, and suffer through ill health, bad relationships, poor finances and emotional upset, than to reach for a greater truth, a higher point of view, a view that encompasses a broader perspective.

How a two-year-old sees the world is much different than how a ten year old sees it. How an eighteen year old sees the world is much different than how a forty year old sees it. The very fact that we no longer see the world as we did when we were two or ten or eighteen, shows that we have changed our points of view, and that means that we have indeed gone through many Transformations. What we think of as lessons in life often leave us with a narrower point of view rather than a more expanded one. We can become more judgmental, more critical and less forgiving. Transformation can often be a shift to a more limiting view of the world, and when it does, it seems to have so much "Rightness" attached to it, that it is difficult to let go of the limiting views.

In 2004 a movie titled "What the Bleep Do We Know" was released and offered the general public an understanding of what Quantum Physicists have been discovering. Half of the movie explains amazing theories of Quantum Physics, and half of the movie follows the life of a woman, and how her life is affected by forces that we generally have not understood. There is a scene in the film where a young man is bouncing a basketball and explaining to the woman that the ball never actually touches the ground. He explains that the electrons of the ball are repelled by the electrons of the pavement, and no particles ever touch other particles. In our so called "Physical Reality" we never touch anything. In the same scene while the woman is looking forward, there are many basketballs bouncing behind her, each representing a possible location of the single basketball. It isn't until she turns around that the actual location of the bouncing ball "Collapses" into a single location and becomes her reality. This "Collapse" is what I would like to focus on.

In an attempt to determine if light travels in waves or particles, scientists developed a test called the "Double-slit experiment." For this test, they took a paper and cut two small slits and placed it in front of a wall. Then using a coherent light source, such as a laser beam, they fired it towards the slits. As the light passed through the slits, it formed a pattern on the wall that was consistent with the light traveling as a wave. This seemed to be quite conclusive that light must travel in waves, but as another part of the experiment, they placed a camera aimed directly at the back side of the slits in order to photograph the individual photons as they emerged from a slit. As soon as the camera was turned on, the wave pattern on the wall changed to a pattern that indicated that the light was somehow now travelling as particles and not waves. When the camera was turned off, the pattern changed back to a wave pattern! This experiment has been replicated over and over with the same result. It seems that light travels in waves until it is observed, and then the wave pattern collapses into individual particles.

Just like with the numerous basketballs bouncing behind the lady in the movie, many possibilities existed for the location of the ball, and it was not until she turned to look or observe the ball that the wave of possibilities collapsed into a single location. This phenomenon is generally referred to as the "collapse of the wave function". As I have pondered this experiment, I can see how it is very similar to how life works. At any moment in time, we have a vast field of possibilities to choose from. It is almost like there is an infinite wave of life moving us forward, and then when we choose an experience, the wave collapses into that single experience, and we are dropped onto a beach or moment of reality. Then we are again back riding the wave to choose the next experience. That wave of life is filled with endless potentials, but for most of us, we keep choosing to ride the same part of the wave and get dropped on the same part of the beach, even though the wave is endless and there are countless areas of beach to land on. The previous choices that we have made create a well worn pattern that keeps us riding that same familiar part of the wave. What we see as possible choices in our future, seem to be guided by the choices that we have made in the past, and the energy of thousands of past choices gives us a limited view of our potential future. We have created patterns of choices that actually obscure the vast possibilities that actually exist as potential future experiences.

Years ago, in the sitcom "Seinfeld," there was a character named George. George was somewhat of an awkward individual, and life just didn't seem to work out very well for him. One day he got the idea that perhaps it was his own "normal" behaviors that were creating his uneventful life, and he decided to make every choice opposite from how he would normally behave. He greeted everyone differently from his normal greeting, he ate differently, he took different routes to get to his destinations, and in a single day his entire life changed. George became a different person by simply making different choices! These new choices had always been available to make, but his history and past behaviors had created a pattern and a vision of who he believed himself to be, and limited his view of his future self.

Picture that after reading this paragraph, you could choose to put the book down and make yourself a meal, or take a shower, or do a meditation, or explore quantum physics on the computer, or realize that you have always been interested in volunteering in your community and take a step towards making that a reality. You could choose to sit and focus on your big toe or on the sound of a bird outside your window. You could pick up the phone and call someone that you have not spoken with in years, to just say hello. You could sit and commit to changing some aspect of your life, or ponder how grateful you are for some ability that you possess. There is literally an infinite amount of choices that you could select from, but we generally will feel the wave of our past pushing us into making familiar choices, being unaware that "Transformation" was available to us in that very moment, and the next moment, and the next moment. An infinite amount of possibilities exist until you choose one and the field collapses into the single choice.

One of the collaborators in the movie "What the Bleep Do We Know" was Dr. Joe Dispenza. If you are not familiar with his work, I highly recommend that you look him up. Dr. Joe, as he is called, has become a Rock Star in the field of Transformation. He has brought in doctors and scientists to study how we develop habits and behaviors, and what it takes to "Transform" or change those habits. There are reasons that we think and feel the way that we do, so what does it take to overcome those reasons or "Points of view?" Do we recognize that there are areas in our lives that we wish were different? Can we continue seeing the world in the same way, and behaving in the same way, and have our lives change, or do we need to adopt a new vision of the world? How would life look if we chose to ride a different part of the wave, and ended up on a completely different area of the beach? As any good surfer could tell you, different parts of the wave move in unique ways, the energy of the wave and movement of the water is different not only in each location, but also in how you approach it and choose to ride it.

Previously we had discussed the works of Dr. David Hawkins and his recognition of the "Levels of Consciousness." Dr. Hawkins's work gives us an amazing tool for recognizing and understanding that there are so many ways of looking at the world; that whatever level of consciousness we are experiencing in the moment affects our vision of the world. Now with the teachings of Dr. Joe Dispenza, we have real tools for reaching higher levels of awareness, and changing how we see and interact with the world. Among the books that Dr. Joe has written, there is YOU ARE THE PLACEBO, BREAKING THE HABIT OF BEING YOURSELF, and BECOMING SUPERNATURAL. These books are filled with the tools for creating your new life, tools for attaining higher levels of consciousness, the very meaning of TRANSFORMATION.

Several days ago, I was having a conversation with a very pleasant young man. He was sharing a story about an incident that took place in a building that was "Known" to be haunted. What appeared to be an apparition or spirit of some sort, had moved across the screen as someone was filming. For this young man, this video was proof that ghosts or spirits exist, and I could sense a slight level of fear coming from him as he related the story to me. He was looking at me, hoping that I might have some bit of information that might support the reality of these ghosts, or at least have some other explanation. For me, this seemed like the perfect time to pull out Dr. Hawkins "Scale of Consciousness." I showed him how the emotion or vibration of fear is at the level of one hundred. Looking at the video evidence of a ghost through the eyes of fear might lead someone to assume that if this ghost is real, it could very well be evil or up to no good. The very presence of a ghost must mean something has gone wrong, and this ghost has not been able to move on to wherever spirits are supposed to go. There was the possibility that ghosts can and do harm us in some way.

Looking at this video through the eyes of Courage, at the level of two hundred, we might see this apparent ghost as interesting, and we might want to know more about it. There is not the immediate worry that we are in danger, nor that if ghosts do exist that we are powerless against them.

If we were to look at this video through the eyes of Love, at the level of five hundred, we might see the possibility of a ghost as wonderful. There is a magic to life and here is proof of some of that magic. In this high vibration, fear cannot exist, in fact, if we were to feel fear, we would instantly stop vibrating at five hundred and we would shift to the level of one hundred, the level of fear.

We have come to know these different vibrations as Emotions, and in labeling them in this way we don't pay attention to how each emotion is just another term for how we vibrate. Because we have words for fear or anger or courage or love, we take these feelings at face value, and don't look for higher understandings. If we really understood that fear was just a particular vibration or frequency, we might feel empowered, knowing that we can change our vibration simply by changing our thoughts.

Since matter does not exist, at least not like we have been led to believe it does, then we might see that everything that we perceive is just a vibration or frequency of energy. Even our thoughts and emotions are just particular frequencies. Our entire existence, including all that we perceive takes place or appears within the infinite field of consciousness. It would be impossible for us to appear outside of this field, yet for many, it is their belief that we are somehow not connected with the field, that we are separate and distinct from it, and it is this feeling of separation that is the cause of all suffering. When we see ourselves as separate, we feel vulnerable and alone. As per Dr. Hawkins view of the levels of consciousness, as we experience Shame we are vibrating at the very low level of just twenty! At this level we feel totally separate from the field and from just about all of life. It is easy to see that as we ascend to each higher level, we feel a little more connected, less alone, and less separate. For most of us, we have become Addicted to our beliefs and emotions, and it might seem nearly impossible to break free of them, and move to a higher vibration, yet it is this letting go of our limited beliefs and points of view, that frees us to experience life in a fuller way.

The experience of Shame is not a bad thing, nor are any emotions Bad, they are part of life and have something to teach us. It is getting stuck in the vibration of shame, and identifying with this vibration as "Who we are" that creates an addiction to shame. Shame becomes part of our identity, and therefore we see the world through the vibration of shame, and this is the vibration that we offer to the world. This is the same for every emotion. We cannot vibrate in "Anger," the level of one hundred fifty, and send ripples of Love into the world. We cannot vibrate in "Guilt," the level of just thirty, and send ripples of Courage into the world.

Dr. Joe Dispenza has offered some great tools for learning how to break free from the habits or addictions that we have developed, that are the very things that are keeping us stuck in our views of the world, and keep us locked in specific vibrations. As with so many spiritual teachings, Dr. Joe utilizes the amazing tool of meditation to retrain the brain to identify vibrations that we have become addicted to, and then to feel what is like to break free of those frequencies, and experience higher levels of consciousness. Dr. Joe has developed some of the most profound meditations that I have personally used to help me reach levels that I had only experienced during Ayahuasca ceremonies. With the help of doctors and scientists, Dr. Joe has used brain scans, heart scans and other instruments to document how as we reach these higher levels of consciousness, our bodies actually respond by releasing natural chemicals that are unparalleled in healing the physical body. These higher states are only accessible by shifting out of the lower vibrations, which means that we are already releasing the thoughts and emotions that had been keeping us locked in our limited view of the world. While in one of these meditations, we are literally working on healing the body and the mind at the same time. By tuning into YouTube and looking up Dr. Joe Dispenza Testimonials, we can listen to hundreds of personal stories of Transformation, stories of people that have used Dr. Joe's work to heal themselves of just about every physical or emotional condition. I have attended one of his Advanced workshops where I witnessed attendees being spontaneously healed from ailments that they had carried since childhood. During one of the meditations, I also experienced a spontaneous healing myself. I had been thrown off a horse at the age of ten, and had suffered damage to both my back and my neck areas. Because of the damage to my back, I had not been able to lie comfortably on my back for at least the past fifteen years. When I would lie on my back, after about one to two minutes I would feel pain in my spine that would increase with every minute that I stayed in that position. I had been seeing chiropractors regularly for about the last thirty years. During one of the meditations at the workshop, as I sat quietly in my chair, focusing on the guided meditation, I suddenly felt three pops in my spine, all at the location of my injury, and then there was such a feeling of release and relief. Since that moment, I have been able to lie on my back for as long as I would like, with no pain!

In many of the testimonials, the people seem to refer specifically to a couple of different meditations that Dr. Joe teaches. Most of the people say that they would use one of these meditations every day, and that they looked forward to every one of those meditations. I would like to share my personal experience using one of these meditations. I have been doing Dr. Joes "Blessing of the Energy Centers III" meditation every morning for several weeks. The meditation is a little over an hour long and focuses on seven energy centers in the body and head and then one center above the head and ends with the energy around the entire body. These centers are also known as chakras. Dr. Joe suggests that we choose a symbol for each energy center, one that would help us focus on a particular emotion or vibration. As an example, many people would choose the symbol of a snake to represent the first or base energy center located at the base of the spine. The snake or serpent might represent the "Kundalini" energy that, when released can climb up the spine creating a profound meditative experience. For my symbol, I chose a strong beautiful wild horse. I would visualize this horse standing or running in a vast meadow. I could feel his power, his freedom and how wonderfully grounded to the Earth he was. As I felt each aspect of this magnificent creature I could feel the vibrations or emotions of freedom, strength and confidence. Each of these vibrations I would experience in my own base center, as though they were my own. As wonderful as these vibrations were, there was also an understanding that each of these were also "Points of View." As strange as it might sound, I understood that in order to actually BE free and not just have the experience of freedom, I needed to surrender my points of view about freedom. In order to BE strong, I needed to surrender my "Points of View" about strength. With each surrender there was a release and an experience of expansion. There would suddenly be Space as though there was now more room to just BE. Another way of explaining the difference between feeling something and being something would be to imagine looking at a pool of beautiful inviting water. We recognize that the pool is there and that the water exists. We might even imagine how the water might feel if we were to jump into the pool. In our meditation, we might step into the pool and actually feel the water as it enveloped our body. We might feel that the water is cool and refreshing as it touches every part of our skin. This is a wonderful feeling as we experience aspects of the water, yet there is still the absolute knowing that even though we are in the water, we are still distinct and separate from it. Then if we were to surrender every point of view about the water and our separateness from it, almost as though a switch were suddenly turned on, we can actually experience being the water. There is no longer a body in the water, there is only the water and our awareness of being. This "Transformation" most likely occurs as we transition from a state of Delta Brain Wave into the deeper level of Gamma. At this level we experience a "Oneness" and an expansion of beingness. We have transitioned from feeling the water, into being the water.

As we moved to the second center, "just below the navel" I would visualize myself as a strong, large Native American man. This man was someone that I had seen in every one of my Ayahuasca ceremonies. I believe that this man had been one of my many incarnations. He was strong and confident. He had been a leader and yet not a Chief. He was respected by everyone in the tribe. He also possessed a wonderful sense of spirit and joy. As I would focus on the vibrations that he inspired of strength, confidence and spiritual connection, I would feel each of these vibrations in my second center, and experience them as if they were my own. Then I would again understand that these were all points of view, and that to actually BE any of these things, I needed to surrender my points of view about them. I could not BE courageous as long as I had points of view about what courage was. As I would surrender these points of view, there was again this experience of expansion and space. I could feel how my own points of view had been keeping me CONTRACTED and releasing them felt like such a gift.

As we moved to the third center, "above the navel and at the base of the gut," I would visualize myself as Mother Teresa. I had been so moved by her words, that as she cared for the poorest of the poor in the slums of Calcutta, she would see "Jesus in all of his many disguises." I would visualize not only people that I had always felt love for, but even those that had caused me the most turmoil in my life, and I would see them as Jesus in disguise. Seeing them in this way, I could only feel the vibrations of Love and Compassion for them, there was no room to feel judgment of them in any way. As wonderful as these feelings were, I was again aware that in order to BE LOVE, and BE COMPASSION, I needed to surrender my points of view about them. Again, as I would surrender, there was the experience of expansion and space. I could experience the freedom from my own limited points of view.

As we moved to the fourth center, "in the middle of the chest," I would visualize Jesus and feel the unconditional love that he would have for everyone, including me. I would open my heart and sense what Jesus was feeling as though the love that he felt was my own. From this view, all that I could feel for any person, animal, plant or any part of creation, was total Love. There didn't seem to be anywhere for negative feelings to hide. As beautiful as this experience was, I understood that I must once again surrender my points of view of Love in order to actually BE LOVE! With this surrender, I was once again experiencing the infinite field of Oneness.

As we moved to the fifth center, "in the middle of the throat," I did not have what I would consider to be a symbol, instead there was the word "Communication." This word symbolized not only verbal communication, but everything from words, body language, deeds, behaviors, work and even art. It included all the ways that we as humans express ourselves. I would look back at the four previous energy centers and understand that how I chose to express myself, must include or be driven by the combined energies of these centers. I could choose to express the highest vibrations of these centers, or I could let lower emotions and habits govern my feelings and actions. I could see how whatever actions or behaviors I chose, would not only define my experience, but would also be the energy that I would "Ripple" through the world. I don't believe that I truly grasped the importance or significance of this energy center, until I had actually done this meditation numerous times. I could see that if I were to be experiencing Fear, Anger, Guilt, Shame or any other lower vibrational states, I could not Ripple Love into the world. We can only share our actual vibration with those around us. We cannot be Angry at a person, situation, political party or even at ourselves and send out anything but that vibration. This center lets us gauge where we are in life. Are we expressing Fear, Grief or Anger, or are we expressing Courage, Acceptance, Love and Joy? To surrender myself into the Infinite Field, through this center, has been Amazing! I understand that every thought and every feeling throughout the day is showing me where I am focusing my attention. We can learn to choose or express any level of vibration that we desire.

As we moved to the sixth center, "at the back of the head," I would visualize myself as Buddha sitting in deep meditation. I could feel the freedom from Earthly concerns and experience a deep peace and joy. My body felt light and expansive, almost as though it was not a physical body made of Matter, but it was a body that seemed to be made from the focusing of the Infinite Field into the Illusion or the symbol of a body. From this meditative state, the entire world was seen as the manifestation of the Infinite Consciousness. All suffering was due to believing that the manifestation was Real, and that we could somehow be separate from the Infinite. It seemed that Buddha had become so attuned to the Infinite Field during meditation, that he was able to maintain that attunement at an almost moment by moment experience of daily life. For me to fully surrender at this stage of my meditation felt so simple and natural. I could easily slip into the Field and become the Infinite.

As we moved to the seventh center, "in the center of the head," I would visualize myself merging with GOD! It seemed as though this was a sacred opening that allowed for a clear, unbiased experience of the creator. Although I have never felt judged by GOD during this merging, I have often felt my own judgments of myself. While in this space, I seemed to be able to see my own human weaknesses from a clear vantage point. I could see that as "physical" beings, we have many perceived needs, some as simple as the need for the air to breathe. Other needs such as food, water and shelter can invoke fear if any of them seem difficult to obtain. Then there are more subjective needs such as companionship, compassion, love and belonging. I could see that we can have so many perceived needs, along with a plethora of emotions if any of these are not met. To be merged or to be one with God, meant that every need disappeared! Even the need for air to breathe seemed to vanish. In this merging, every "normal" human emotion became irrelevant. The only feeling that was noticeable was that of Love, but even that could not be described as a feeling or emotion. It was instead more like Love was the experience of being whole. In the state of oneness, there literally was nothing to be separate from, and without separateness there was only wholeness and Love. I understood that God or the infinite consciousness would never have judgments of me: only I could have judgments of myself while experiencing separation from the whole.

As we moved to the eighth center, "just above the head," I would visualize the most beautiful giant crystal floating in the infinite void. This was my symbol for how the infinite consciousness would focus the light of human life through the crystal and just like light going through a prism, the light of human life would be split into the different energy centers creating a divided soul. With this division came the experience of separation. The one true light divided itself into different colors, each appearing to be separate and distinct from each other. Even though each color seemed to have its own flavor or feeling, I understood that not only were they each still part of the whole but that this was only a way of perceiving or experiencing separation. In truth, separation from the infinite is just not possible, but the PERCEPTION of separation is essential for the human experience. Another way of looking at the division of light, would be to interpret each light as a vibration, and each vibration would experience life from a different perspective. Just like putting on a pair of green colored glasses would change your vision of the world, so would having a vibration or frequency of red in your root center. Having multiple colors, vibrations or frequencies as energy centers would provide for different ways of viewing or experiencing human life. We could focus, or "stand" in our red root center, also referred to as the survival center, and perhaps experience life through the eyes of fear. Or we could focus or "stand" in our fourth center, also referred to as the "heart" center, and view the world through the vibration of Love or Joy. The division of light allows us to interpret the world from different perspectives. Each light lets us stand and view the world through a completely different pair of glasses. How we feel about the world and our place in it, is direct evidence of which energy center we are viewing from.

As we moved to the final Area, the field around the entire body, I would visualize my body floating in the vast void and sense that the entire infinite space was somehow being focused into my body, almost as though the body was a manifestation of the field, being supported by the field, and being loved by the infinite. From this perspective, I could sense the body as a whole again, not just from the separate centers, but it was now a complete unit with every part and every center working together. At the same time, I felt totally connected to the infinite field, even feeling nurtured and cared for. The final step in the meditation was to bring this completeness back and almost condensing it into my human form, leaving me in a state of such fullness and joy, that there are just no words to adequately describe.

This meditation has been profound in helping me to experience and understand myself in ways that had somehow eluded me through years of using many different meditation techniques. The symbols that I have chosen to use for each of my energy centers have worked for me. I hope that everyone finds powerful symbols that work for them. We are all unique and will respond to each word or symbol in our own unique way. Also, I can attest to the effectiveness of using this meditation EVERY DAY. It is as though each meditation builds on the ones before. I have looked forward to each morning, knowing that I am going be visiting the infinite and bringing back magical awarenesses.

This chapter deals with "Transformation," and this meditation can be a wonderful vehicle for Transforming beliefs and understandings, giving us new ways of viewing the world, and how we fit into it. Dr. Joe Dispenza has found and developed some of the most powerful tools for helping us Transform our lives, healing us physically, emotionally and psychologically. Most often, we believe that we need the world to change in order for us to be happy, but using meditation as a tool, we begin to understand that true happiness can only be found in our own personal Transformation. There is nothing outside of us that can ever be a consistent source of Joy and Peace.

Story #22-What is attention

Years ago, my wife had taught a class on consciousness. One of the topics was "Your attention is the currency with which you buy your life." It was one of my favorite classes and that particular topic seemed to make so much sense. If we place our attention on something negative, then for as much time as we choose to keep our focus there, we are literally trading our time (our life) for a negative experience. For every minute that we spend worrying, we are trading our time for the experience of worry. Is it possible that simply by choosing to place our attention on only pleasant or joyful things, our lives would be filled with joy? Would it be possible to only focus on pleasant thoughts when the outer world seems to be filled with so many "negative" events? Is it silly to believe that we could change our experience of life simply by choosing to pay attention to where we place our attention?

So now years later, it occurred to me, that as with all words we think we know what that word means. Perhaps the word "attention" has more meaning to it than my limited point of view had included. I wondered for instance, was attention what I might be looking at, what I might be feeling, or what I might be thinking? Does attention have to do with what the brain is perceiving, what consciousness is perceiving or what all my physical senses are perceiving? According to Wikipedia, "Attention is the behavior and cognitive process of selectively concentrating on a discrete aspect of information, whether considered subjective or objective, while ignoring other perceivable information. It is a state of arousal." It almost sounds as if they are saying that attention is a tool, something that can be used to select what we want to experience. If we were to be driving down a country road, we could be placing our attention on the beautiful hills, trees and abundance of life; or we could place our attention on how fast we could move on an open road; or we could place our attention on our destination, and not even notice the landscape. Where we choose to put our attention changes our entire experience!

As I thought about asking my guide for a definition of attention, I wondered if it would be a fair question. After all, attention is just a word and it is open to many different interpretations. There was at some point in time, someone that came up with the word attention and gave it a meaning. Perhaps all that original meaning was to say look over here, or listen to me. Most likely the inventor of the word did not ponder that attention might mean the very essence of who we are! So if the inventor of the word did not make the meaning of it crystal clear, how could I ask my guide to give me the "correct" definition?

So I sit quietly in meditation and ask my guide, "What is attention?" I can feel my normal mind trying to give answers, and have to quiet those thoughts, and give space for the deeper experience to come. Soon the information begins to flow; it starts by the realization that in order to even contact my guide or pose the question about attention, I must focus that very thing called attention on looking for a response. I see that the physical world around me seeks my attention. I can hear the sounds of the ravens outside my window. I can feel that my body is somewhat uncomfortable sitting in the chair. The light in the room and the light of the computer screen are difficult to ignore. I am aware of my body asking to be fed my morning smoothie. I can taste that I have not yet brushed my teeth. Then there are all the normal thoughts that come into awareness and then disappear again only to be replaced by other thoughts.

It literally seems that there are thousands of places that I could choose to place my attention, each one saying "hey, look at me." Fortunately, I have practiced the art of meditating and I have a path to focus on, to leave all these voices behind. It is almost like dropping into a vast well that has walls that block out the intruding thoughts, and yet expands into infinite space. I begin to explore the vastness that is the true self. Who I am, is awareness itself; awareness being unlimited, without borders or end. In the depths of awareness, time and space have little meaning. Who is the I, that is choosing to place this thing called attention? I become aware that what I call my mind is just a filter that the larger self uses to interact in this physical reality.

In the larger picture, all that exists is Awareness. Some may refer to awareness as God or All That Is, or the Everything; but for our conversation, I will be using the word Awareness. All form or what we call matter, is a manifestation of Awareness. Without Awareness, there could be no form. Without Awareness, there would be no Attention or anything to focus attention on. Awareness is truly the beginning and the end; it is both the created and the creator; it is the form and the perceiver of the form.

Attention is the focusing of Awareness. The BIG question is WHO is doing the focusing? We might instinctively say that "I" am doing the focusing; that I am choosing what I am focusing on. If Awareness is all that is, and nothing exists outside of Awareness, and all form is a manifestation of Awareness, then "I" must also be a manifestation of Awareness! I am in a way Awareness perceiving itself, but from a very unique perspective, (The perspective of the individual "I" that is who I believe myself to be.) We as humans are each aspects of Awareness perceiving other aspects or manifestations of Awareness. We each represent unique ways or points from which "All That Is" can be experienced. There are no two people that see or could ever see the world in the exact same way. Our unique vibrations and our life experiences give different understandings of life and of the world. We each Stand and view the world from our very own unique vantage point. It is not possible to separate yourself from Awareness. Without Awareness, there could not be a knowing or recognition of a self.

If I am indeed Awareness or an aspect of Awareness, then I must also be the focusing of that Awareness. I must be Attention, and I am the focus of Awareness that is seeing or experiencing life from this vantage point that is called "I." I think this, I see it this way, I feel like this. The very I that is me, is the focusing of Awareness into a Point of View. My Attention is the focusing of my point of view on an aspect or manifestation of Awareness. In a very real sense, Attention is more like what I am, rather than what I am doing.

If Attention is truly the focusing of who or what I am, then how valuable is my attention? Why would I choose to focus on or view anything from a negative place? Why would I choose to spend my time, my life, my gift of experience, focusing on anything that was not in the highest vibration of Love? If Love is the very essence of Awareness, and my attention is an aspect of Awareness, then it must be my Birthright to be able to experience or vibrate at the level of Love, no matter where or what I am perceiving. Why would I ever allow what I am perceiving or focusing on to lower my vibration below the vibration of Love?

Perhaps the answer to that question involves this thing we call the Ego. Perhaps it is the ego that has a stake in being Right and can feel injured, or even believe that its very existence is in question when it might be found to be Wrong.

The ego may actually believe that being Wrong is worse than death itself. In order for the ego to maintain its "Rightness" about a perception or belief, it is willing to lower its vibration to that of Pride, or Anger, or even Fear, just to avoid being perceived as "Wrong."

Perhaps it is focusing Attention through the eyes of Ego that allows us to experience anything below the level of the vibration of Love. Without our higher vibration going through some type of filter; something that has the power to change that vibration, then we would always maintain our higher level of Love. I am not implying that the ego is a bad or negative thing, I am only saying that we must be alert as to the activity and power of the ego. When we are experiencing any of the lower vibrations, we are perceiving life or aspects of life through a lens that is obscuring or altering the true nature of our experience. The ego is literally adding a flavor or view of our experience that does not allow for the expression of Love in that experience.

If Attention is the focusing of who we are, then the value of attention is the value of self. There is nothing that we possess that could be of more value, and yet we are often willing to give our attention to things that are of no benefit to the magnificent beings that we are. If we truly grasp the incredible wonder of Attention, and understood how beautiful and precious it is, we would not want to waste a minute of life with our Attention filtered through the eyes of ego into the depths of the lower vibrations. To be vigilant as to where and how our Attention is focused is to honor ourselves and honor All That Is. Perhaps this is what being Enlightened means.

I have often wondered about value. Of what value is a single human life, and who would be finding value in that life? It may seem obvious that a parent would value the life of their child, or someone would value the life of a friend. In fact, value could be found in any relationship, from family, friends, work, school or community; but I wondered if the value of a life could be so much more than these relationships. Could my life and the lives of every person have more meaning, more purpose and be of more value than I had ever considered? Could life itself serve a purpose that goes beyond what might seem evident?

Many people have reported that while experiencing an NDE or Near Death Experience, they found themselves in an infinite black void. They described this void as complete "Nothingness" without physical or energetic properties. They seemed to be fully conscious and have a complete sense of self, knowing that they existed and seemed to be able to "move around" in the void. Some have reported feeling as though they spent what seemed like years in this place of blackness. With nothing to be in relationship with, could such a life still have value? As I pondered this question, I could feel that without a doubt even a life in such a void still had Purpose. To be in the void but still be aware was still the very essence of life. Awareness is the beginning and the end, (if there is such a thing as the end.) Without Awareness, even the void would not exist, without Awareness there would be no Value.

When we speak of Awareness, we don't say we have Aware, we say we ARE Aware. No matter where we are standing, whether in a city, on a beach, in a church, in the countryside, in a dream, or even in the infinite Void, we are ALWAYS AWARE.

As I thought about these people floating in the void, I pictured myself floating there in the emptiness all alone. I wondered if while floating there, could I dream? Would it be possible to dream of a planet full of people? Would it be possible to dream of an entire Universe? How many dreams could I have? How many places could I create? How many Relationships could I experience? If all there was in this vast blackness was ME, MY Awareness, the Knowing that I AM, how long would it take me to master the art of Dreaming? If I am AWARE, could I choose what I wanted to be aware of? Making a choice would be to decide to place Attention on my creation.

I thought about how every aspect of a dream is created by me. I might create a mountain, a building, a city, a sky, a lake, hundreds of people, a monster, a bear, a forest or anything that can be dreamed of. No matter what is in my dream, it was created by me. Usually there would be a character in the dream that would be the center of attention. This character would generally represent ME, and I would experience the dream through the eyes, mind and filters of that character. I remember having many dreams where I would be a certain character and seeing the dream through their eyes, but suddenly I would also experience parts of the dream through the eyes of some of the other characters. I might for instance be a man being chased by a bear; I would feel fear and be running for my life, and then suddenly I would also be experiencing being the bear chasing the man. I would feel the power and strength of the bear and see the man running in front of me. I wondered how many characters or aspects of the dream could I place my Attention on, and experience the same dream from a different perspective? In fact, since every aspect of the dream is my creation, could I experience the dream from the perspective of the lake, and feel the peace of the water, or the sky, and feel the expanse of the space, or from all of it at once? Is it possible that by placing my Attention on one thing rather than another, I am choosing what my experience will be? Could I experience a forest from the view of a tree, or experience the tree from the view of a leaf?

If I am floating in the infinite void, would I choose to experience black nothingness, or would I choose to explore the infinite possibilities of dreams? Would I place my Attention on empty space, or would I choose to place my Attention on what I might be able to create? Every creation springs forth from the infinite Nothingness. It is from the infinite void that all manifestation begins, every dream begins somewhere. In the void, all possibilities exist. Everything that can be dreamed can only begin in Awareness, without Awareness, there are no dreams, no manifestations, no universe and no thoughts. Whether we call it God, Awareness, The Everything, or All That Is, everything that can ever be manifested, created or experienced is already contained in the infinite void. Although floating in this infinite blackness may seem as though there is nothing, there is also everything. It is Attention that is the focus of Awareness, and that gives us what we perceive as our experience. Attention is the gift that we are. It is our Ego, our thoughts, beliefs and filters that give the perception of limits; these are the things that can lower the frequency of our vibration and give us an unpleasant view of life.

What if it was possible to learn to dream better, to learn to dream in a way that would allow for a richer, happier and more productive life? What if there was a way of learning to use Attention to create a broader view and understanding of the beings that we seem to be? It is possible to program a dream, to influence what we dream and how aware we might become in that dream! As we lie in bed ready to fall asleep, we might give ourselves instructions to have a flying dream, to experience the freedom from gravity and have the ability to fly above the trees. By picturing ourselves soaring above the buildings, the people and the landscape, we are actually giving our subconscious minds the instructions to experience such a dream. By telling ourselves over and over, that if we find ourselves in such a dream where we are actually flying, that we will recognize that we are in fact dreaming. As we are experiencing this dream of flying and we recognize that we are in a dream, we can bring more conscious awareness into the dream, almost to the point of experiencing the dream with our waking consciousness. We are still dreaming and able to fly, but now we understand that we are in control of the dream. We can choose where we fly, how fast we fly, and how much joy we want to experience while flying. We have successfully programmed our dream to give us an experience of our choosing, rather than a random dream created by the subconscious mind.

As we become more aware that our Reality is very much like a dream, then we in fact have the ability to become more awake in that dream. We become more Enlightened and bring a higher level of consciousness into our perceived reality. The things in life that we may have found to be frightening, can now be seen from a higher perspective, a higher vibration, and the fear may be transformed into appreciation or maybe even Love. As a character in the dream, we may become aware that this is a dream, but we still may not really understand Who is doing the dreaming. Just because we understand that we are dreaming, we don't suddenly have access to the reality of the dreamer. The dream is still continuing and keeps most of the focus of Attention on the dream, but as we become aware that this is a dream, the focus of "Attention" is expanded, and the Reality of the dream is perceived from a larger perspective. From this new perspective, we recognize that we have far more influence over our surroundings, and in fact we may begin to understand that every aspect of our surroundings has meanings that have not been seen or understood before.

Generally speaking, as a dreamed character, we are not aware that every aspect of the dream has been and is being created by the same dreamer that is creating us. From the view of the dreamed character, everything in the world seems solid and real. Every person and creature seem to be real and separate from us. As we increase our level of awareness, we begin to vibrate at higher frequencies and the illusion of the separate self begins to dissipate. We begin to feel more connected and more expanded. This feeling of expansion is almost always accompanied by the higher levels of consciousness, such as Acceptance, Love, Peace or Joy. At these higher levels, we recognize that our Attention has been expanded and is no longer focused on the limiting views of the Ego. Our view of the world is richer and clearer, with the old views of separation fading away. Our Attention has expanded almost as though we had stepped back from the world and can see it from a larger perspective.

For most of us, our present moment is defined by the memories of our past; our Attention is focused on the path that led up to this moment. We remember the Somebody training that we received since infancy. We remember the moments that limited our beliefs in our own abilities, our talents and our view of what we might become. We have slowly agreed to the limits and definitions of who and what we believe we are. This also means that our future is viewed through these same limitations. We have used the unlimited power of our Attention to create a very limited self. We do this by focusing our Attention on the stories that we have heard throughout our lives and believing them to be true. For each of the stories that we have accepted as "the way it is," there were so many other ways of seeing or interpreting each of them. The following is a story that was shared by one of my many teachers.

There was a poor family that lived in a small town in a small country. They had been fortunate enough to have been able to purchase a rather nice-looking horse that they used to help plow the field. One day the horse disappeared, and their neighbor finding out about what had happened, exclaimed "What a shame; that is so sad." The farmer, being a wise man, simply replied, "You never know." The next day the horse returned with a magnificent stallion following her. The neighbor, seeing the new horse said, "Praise the Lord, you are so fortunate." The wise farmer simply replied, "You never know." The farmer's son decided one day that he would tame this wild horse. After struggling to get a saddle on the horse, he mounted the stallion, and was very quickly thrown to the ground, breaking his arm as he landed. The neighbor upon hearing the story, exclaimed, "How terrible, what an unfortunate thing to happen." The farmer once again replied, "You never know." A couple of days later, a group of soldiers arrived at the farm, looking to recruit any able-bodied young men for a war against the neighboring country. Seeing the farmer's son with the broken arm, they determined that he was not of value, and left the farm without him.

We interpret every event in our own unique way, often calling this event good and another event bad; but what if every event was supposed to happen? What if somewhere hidden in everything that happens, there is a message, a gift, a new way of seeing life? What if instead of judging, labeling or viewing life from our very limited perspective, we accepted that every event is unfolding just the way that we need in order to give us the opportunity for spiritual evolvement? Acceptance of what is, frees us from resistance, and allows us to say, "this is where I am at, where do I go from here."

Instead of placing our Attention on resisting present circumstances, we are free to place our Attention on this moment as though it is a fresh start. We do not bring the weight of the past into this moment, or into the future. Acceptance is key to freeing the future from the limits of the past.

Attention is indeed the very power that we are. Where we place our Attention and the energy or story that we place behind that "Attention," brings us our experience of each moment. We can choose to place our Attention on what appears to be a negative event or situation and support those negative thoughts and feelings with stories from our past; or we could see every event and situation as a new experience, and look for what gifts or opportunities they may show us. The Ego wants to keep us locked in the past and viewing all events and situations through its eyes. The Ego will run thought after thought through our minds, telling us, showing us, reminding us that we are Right to see this situation in a negative way. It is being locked in the negative view, and the belief in our Rightness that keeps us in the lower levels of consciousness. It is only when we are Willing to expand our views and go beyond the past and the EGO, that we can move up to the higher levels of Awareness.

The higher levels of Awareness are another way of saying that we have expanded our Attention and are able to view our reality from a much larger perspective. We have achieved some level of freedom from our past and from the Ego. We are able to experience the present moment with an expanded sense of being that enables us to see a greater level of truth. It is always through the process of surrender, that Attention is allowed to grow, or more accurately, we allow ourselves to experience greater levels of Attention, by the very act of surrender.

I have had the pleasure of experiencing life from many levels of Awareness and from many levels of Consciousness. I have felt my spirit take wings while experiencing levels of Gratitude, Love, Joy and Appreciation. I have travelled in meditations with my guide to levels of Awareness that seemed to have included higher dimensions and planes of existence where I have barely had memory of my physical self. With the help of Ayahuasca, I have travelled beyond the physical, and even to the edge of creation itself. There have also been those amazing times that I was able to shed my ego enough to lose every point of view and experience oneness.

Perhaps being able to have a point of view is God's gift to us. What we do with that point of view is our gift to God. The more we become stuck in our rightness about our Points of View, the greater we separate ourselves from the whole truth, from the All Knowing and from the Creator.

Epilogue

Although each of these stories has been lived and experienced by me during this single lifetime, it feels as though most of them took place a lifetime ago! As I look back at my life, it often seems like events happened to a different me, a person that I used to be, or perhaps they had been viewed through eyes that no longer fit the me that I am today. In recalling and writing down each of these stories, I relived them through my present eyes and my hopefully more expanded awareness. It seemed as though I gained understanding of each of these experiences that had somehow escaped my awareness when they actually took place. Writing these stories down literally changed my life and helped me to gain knowledge of myself and my place in this physical reality.

There are now somewhere around eight billion people on the planet, each of us unique, and experiencing this reality from our own perspective. Each perspective is one hundred percent true, and valid, from a very limited, and unique point. I believe that we are each here to explore and express light and love, although often it may not appear that way. Our minds, egos, and life's teachings, seem to get in the way of how we interpret and express that love. Often our expressions appear to be contrary to what we think of as love. Our limited understanding of what love is and how it may be expressed, keep us from recognizing how we are all calling out for that love, and trying to find ways of deserving it.

In this reality, we cannot know the WHY of things; the structure of all the circumstances that have created our present moment. Without knowing or understanding the deeper WHY, we are left with trusting that everything is happening just the way that it is supposed to. Are we able to see the perfection in all the things that seem so imperfect? In so many of my dreams, I was in mortal combat with creatures of the dark, and so often I seemed unable to defeat them. Over and over it seemed that the lesson I was learning was that it was silly to do battle, when I could rise above the creatures and fly into the safety of the sky. The view of the creatures from the sky gave me the understanding of how limited the powers of these creatures were, and how our battles could only take place when I would drop down to their level. During the battles and struggles, I would be so focused on the creatures and my situation that I seemed to have forgotten that I had the power and ability to fly. I always had that ability, but life has a way of making us forget. It is only when we change how we SEE a situation that we recognize our own power. Our POWER is not in changing the things around us, it is in the ability to change how we view those things. As we change how we view life, WE CHANGE.

When we are born into this physical reality, we are thrust into a PERCEIVED place of separation from ALL THAT IS. We have a physical body that seems separate from the world around us. We have legs that seem separate from our arms. We have organs that seem separate from our blood, and as we go deeper into the human form, we see even more separation. We have separate cells that can be divided into other separate parts. We have DNA that is unique and separate from every other human's DNA. As we go deeper, we see that even the cells and parts of the cells and even the DNA, are made of even smaller things like molecules and then atoms. It appears that our levels of separation have no limits. We come from an infinite field where separation has little meaning, into this place where separation seems to rule everything. Our five senses tell us that we are indeed separate from every other thing in this world, yet if we continue down the "Rabbit Hole," past the cells, the molecules and the atoms; as we go deeper into what we are made of; we move past the tiniest of things and end up right back in the infinite void! We end up back where all Creation begins.

A student once asked his master, " What is real?" The master replied, "That which does not change is real." Yet as we look at our perceived physical reality, we see that everything changes. We change, and every form of life is changing. The Earth is ever changing, as is the Sun, the galaxy and all of the known Universe. In fact perhaps the one thing that does not change is the very fact that everything is changing. Nothing in our reality seems to stay the same. Does that mean that nothing is real; or could it mean that everything is real?

Some have said that AWARENESS, GOD, or ALL THAT IS, is the one true constant; it is only INFINITE AWARENESS that does not change. Yet if our personal experiences, our triumphs and sorrows don't have an effect on INFINITE AWARENESS, then what would be the point of our very existence? Without change, there could be NO EXPERIENCE! Even floating in the infinite void without a body, our very awareness is EXPERIENCE; and that knowing of experience is CHANGE!

In this physical reality, every one of our experiences changes how we perceive ourselves and our world. The greatest power that we possess is that we have a choice on how we allow each experience to change us. Do we choose to see each experience in ways that advance our understanding of Love; or do we choose to use these experiences to reinforce old and limiting views? Even my meditation that brought me into the depths of the Earth, Matter and perhaps even what we might think of as Hell, can be seen through the eyes of Love, and uplift our spirits to higher frequencies and vibrations. In every traumatic event that occurs, whether it is the loss of a loved one, a natural catastrophe, a financial loss, or a personal transgression, there is the opportunity to expand our understanding of Love, or to contract into our old views. Perhaps FREE WILL is not so much about the ability to choose a path, as it is about the ability to choose how we see that path. Perhaps it is more about choosing which eyes we use to see every event, every person, ourselves, and life. Are we using the eyes of LOVE, or the eyes of other lower vibrational levels of awareness?

Every experience seems to have this DICHOTMY, where it can be viewed and experienced from the lower consciousness levels, such as guilt or shame, and make us feel smaller, injured or less whole; or it can be viewed and experienced from a higher level, such as love or joy, and make us feel lighter, expanded, and more connected. We tend to believe that an experience should be the same for everyone. As an example, let's say that you are walking down a sidewalk, and not paying attention, and you accidentally run into a light post. You are startled and look around to see if anyone was watching. You notice that there were some people across the street that had indeed seen it all and are looking at you. You may feel stupid and embarrassed, and want to get away as quickly as possible; or you could enjoy the moment, see it as funny, and be happy that others were able to see it and join in the silliness of the situation. The single event has no meaning of its own. The only meanings are those that we bestow upon them. We choose how we see the event, and we choose how we see ourselves and life in relation to that event.

When we begin to question what in this world is real, and what is reality itself, we invite the mystical into our life. By our very questions, we are asking the universe to show itself, and peek out from the illusion of the material world. We must be open to what it reveals, as our old beliefs are challenged and discarded. We must be open to expanding our awareness, rather than looking to define it. Reality is always ready for us to expand into its infinite possibilities. It has no agenda that desires to keep us from knowing or experiencing its magnificence. It is only our fears of letting go of our very limited views that keep us from seeing a greater truth.

I had been blessed with the opportunity to share much of my life with the most wonderful woman. She was gifted with the ability to help people see life in a more expanded way. One of the many beautiful gifts she shared with me was when a difficulty or challenge showed up in my life, I should stop and ask, "What would Love do now?" What energy do I want to address the challenge with? Working with the frequencies of Hate, Anger, Fear, Anxiety or Guilt, would be abandoning the magnificent tools of Love, Joy and Peace. We can accomplish so much more using our best tools.

It is absolutely my belief that Everything we do changes the entire world. Every action that we take sends Ripples into the world, leaving our signature or footprint with it. What Ripples do we want to send? What do we want our legacy to be? Freewill means that we have the choice as to how we see the world, and what tools or frequencies we are going to Ripple into that world. Every day, every situation, every moment is a new opportunity to express Love in our own unique way.

May your Ripples be filled with Love, Joy and Peace.

Endnotes

---

[i] Edward Lorenz-questioned whether a butterfly flapping its wings in one place could lead to a tornado a continent away.

[ii] Both the name of the class and the name of the instructor have been changed.

[iii] The Naked Scientists 5-17-2016

[iv] Ram Dass Lecture, "Nowhere to Stand" 4-30-2015

Note-At the time that I wrote Story #17-The Quantum Self, many of the science websites agreed with "The Naked Scientists" regarding the number of cells in a human fetus at birth. Since the writing of this story, most of the other sites have drastically altered their calculations.